# purpose power

## HOW MISSION-DRIVEN LEADERS
## ENGAGE FOR CHANGE

# ALICIA BONNER NESS

ONBrand Books

Published by ONBrand Books
(an imprint of W. Brand Publishing, Nashville, TN)

j.brand@wbrandpub.com
www.wbrandpub.com

Cover design: JuLee Brand / designchik.net

Ordering Information:
Quantity sales. Special discounts are available on quantity purchases by corporations, associations, and others. For details, contact the "Special Sales Department" at the email address above.

Purpose Power / Alicia Bonner Ness. —1st ed.

Hardcover ISBN: 978-1-950385-08-9
Paperback ISBN: 978-1-950385-01-0
eBook ISBN: 978-1-950385-02-7

Library of Congress Control Number: 2019935434

# contents

*This book is dedicated to Rachel Lorfils, Nadia McBean, Lizbeth Moreno, Vanessa Romero, and all of the other dedicated volunteers of south Florida who showed up tirelessly and consistently to do the grueling work that mattered most. Most especially, it is dedicated to Marilyn Frisch, whose unflagging commitment to democracy and justice motivates me every single day.*

# THE LAST MILE

The moment has come. You can go no further.

There is nothing left. You are ready to quit.

Yet it is not yet over. You have not yet sealed the deal, closed the loop, won the race. In the marathon, it is mile 25. You cannot believe how far you have come, how hard you have fought, and how far you still have left to go. And yet nothing has changed. All that blood, sweat, and tears, and the score is still 0–0 with five minutes (or fifteen days) left to play.

Despite the lack of apparent progress, you cannot quit.

You are so ready to throw in the towel, but you have fought too hard to die here. Not on this hill. Athletes, soldiers, organizers—these are the moments that test our mettle, our courage, our commitment. These moments depend on the foundation, the support structure, you have built under you, your practiced endurance. Have you run enough sprints to keep going when the gas light is flashing bright red, when the wheels are ready to come off, when the train is about to jump the tracks? Can you trust yourself and those around you to look inside, to dig deep, and to find the steely grit to give more than you have left? To trust adrenaline to carry you when you know you are running on fumes?

In this moment, the options are certain failure or possible victory. You can tap out or stay for the coin flip, knowing you could give everything and lose everything, too.

You will wake up today and climb out of the foxhole and onto the battlefield. Mark one more hash on the wall to honor one more day burning past empty. Such moments drive us to faith and to prayer. They lead us to question ourselves and our smallness on this planet. Is it intended that you are here on purpose to do this work?

These moments are the seeds of legends in the making, a story only you can write. You are the field marshal, the last-mile reconnaissance officer, and the sergeant all at once. You are the maker of legend in a proverbial tomorrow, where the world's future rests in your hands.

Give today what you do not have left and it shall be returned to you a hundred-fold.

Go forth, lone warrior. Chase that last mile. Go ahead. Make history.

–*Alicia Bonner Ness, October 2016*

# INTRODUCTION

On the morning of November 9, 2016, the world felt both exactly the same and dramatically different from how it had the day before. Where once there was hope, it was tempting to feel both skepticism and despair. If I'd had one ounce of energy left, I might have felt rage. Instead, the morning after the election of Donald Trump as the 45th president of the United States of America, I sat engulfed in deep, aching sadness. How was it possible for so many people—including me—to have worked so hard, and still lose?

I had spent the months before Election Day working as a field organizer for the Florida Democratic Party in Broward County, registering voters, and turning them out to vote. The choice to join the Clinton campaign was both premeditated and random. I had always hoped to help elect America's first female president. I had no idea that this aspiration would lead me to spend the weeks before Election Day working fourteen-hour days knocking doors in the most crucial battleground state. I couldn't yet fathom how this choice would reshape the arc of my life.

In the weeks that followed, I thought deeply about why we had lost. What had we missed, I wondered? How could it be that so many people could exert such exceptional effort and meet defeat? We know now far more than we knew then about the efforts of bad actors to influence the psychology of American voters and stoke feelings of anger and distrust in key areas of the United States, especially in Florida, though, as of this writing, the full story of how the 2016 election was manipulated has not yet been revealed.[1] As I reflected on the outcome, I realized that the challenges that had hampered the success of Hillary Clinton's campaign were the same challenges many mission-driven organizations face in their pursuit of impact.

## Three Obstacles to Mission-Driven Impact

After spending ten years in the social sector developing brand strategies and fundraising campaigns on behalf of nonprofits, I had some experience with the challenges mission-driven organizations face. Three problems in particular yield inertia and inefficacy.

The first is confirmation bias, the tendency to interpret new evidence as confirmation of one's existing beliefs. In marketing and communication, just as much as in community organizing, this allows leaders to insist that the thing that has always worked will continue to work, in spite of overwhelming evidence to the contrary. In 2008, the Obama campaign was ahead of the Republican Party in its use of technology. By 2016, the Hillary Clinton campaign assumed the same advantage was still at play. Once you have come to expect an approach to work the way it always has, organizations often have to learn the hard way that the paradigm has shifted, yielding diminishing returns.

Second, in most organizations that run on shoestring budgets where every dollar counts (both nonprofits and political campaigns), most people are underpaid. Everyone is overworked. This combination of circumstances yields an overwhelming "house-on-fire" environment that drives you to default to the "tried-and-true" solution your confirmation bias insists will work, again, in spite of overwhelming evidence to the contrary. Urgency stymies efforts to consider new alternatives, instead insisting that people simply put their heads down and do the work—you can ask questions later.

The third challenge arises when confirmation bias and the house-on-fire conspire against you. Taken together, the "do-it-now!" mandate paired with a clear default option makes it even more likely people will miss the most critical question: Why are we doing this? It can be tempting to assume that we are all equally passionate about the same things, inspired for the same reasons, pulling in the same direction, because we are all hoping for the same happy ending. This assumption, as they say, makes an ass of all of us.

## A Different Tack

In many ways, the Special Counsel's investigation into Russian interference in the 2016 election has diverted animus and attention away from a thorough and searching after-action review. Instead of looking at the popular vote—yes,

Hillary Clinton got two million *more* votes than Donald Trump, and the Special Counsel's indictments—yes, Russia *did* attempt to interfere—and chalking up our loss to bad luck, I decided to take a different tack.

Political campaigns are the flimsiest of endeavors. Like the circus, they seem to appear with great fanfare and disappear overnight. Though fleeting, when done well, they still manage to stoke the ire and inspiration of the masses. So, what is it that makes them work? In 2016, both Bernie Sanders and Donald Trump had clarity of ideological conviction that Hillary Clinton's campaign lacked. Your advocates must clearly understand the shared beliefs that underpin your mission. This knowledge provides a critically important foundation for impact that many organizations both inside and outside of the political arena de-prioritize or postpone to their detriment.

In the months following the election, I set out to define a framework that could help mission-driven organizations of all stripes inspire their advocates to engage for change. The result is the Heptagon Method, the foundation of this book. Rather than haphazardly using tactics that respond to the fire that flames up on any particular day, it offers a clear series of steps that lead to results. My hope is that the structure of what to do first, and what to do next will help you quickly answer the question, "What do we do now?" I also hope that this framework will protect you from defaulting to the safe option you have always relied on and allow you to imagine new possibilities. Most importantly, perhaps, this framework is based on a starting point of ideological clarity, from which you can clearly understand—and articulate—why your mission motivates engagement.

Different people will find different value in this book. If you are confused about what ideological clarity is and why it matters, consider starting with Chapter 3. If you are setting out to rebrand your organization, you will find inspiration in Chapters 4 and 5. Stories are a singularly effective marketing tool; to find out why they work and how to tell them, read Chapter 6. If you are setting out to produce a large-scale event, you will find nuggets of wisdom packed into Chapter 7. If a strong community already anchors your organization, consider starting with Chapter 8 to discover how to inspire your advocates to engage for change. Finally, if you have questions about action—how to raise money, increase visibility, or sell product—you will probably benefit from first reading Chapter 10, which illustrates how it all hangs together, and why first things must come first. You will, however, find tactical advice on action in Chapter 9, which offers insight into how to inspire your advocates to take action toward your shared vision.

I spent the weeks and months that followed the 2016 election wavering between being motivated to get up and do something, anything, to improve my little corner of the universe, and unproductively wallowing in despair. This book is my attempt to offer a pathway for progress out of circumstances that can feel insurmountable. A few of the examples in this book will be about brands you have never heard of, but it is my conviction that personal experience is the best teacher. I hope that my reflections and insights can support you on your journey to lead the change you believe our world needs, one step at a time.

## Three Important Lessons

Three core lessons for mission-driven brands stand at the heart of this book. The first is the importance of having rock-solid brand foundations. You have to understand your ideology and have a vibrant identity that supports it. You have to understand your audience and how to inspire your advocates. If you try to rush to event planning or fundraising without these fundamentals in place, you may not fail, but you are unlikely to achieve your desired results.

Second, recognize the power stories and experiences have to inspire people. Get people together in a room. Tell them about the human impact of your work. Do not rely on raw statistics to convince people of facts. Stories in any media— recorded or live—are the most powerful tools you have to persuade people to share your vision and support your cause.

Most importantly, perhaps, embrace the need for change. As scary and uncomfortable as it may be, change is ever-present. It is the beating heart of what makes us human, animal, alive. Rather than staying stuck in the ugly awkwardness of this moment, you have the power to move the needle. So do it. Set your eye on the horizon. Articulate your conviction, and get started putting that vision into action.

I spent a lot of my life waiting to get picked, for the perfect opportunity to present itself. Perhaps you, too, have spent a great deal of your life waiting for someone to tap you on the shoulder and invite you into a secret change-making club that will reveal the secrets of radical impact. I hate to be the bearer of bad news, but that day will never come. It is up to you to define your future and to find the grit and determination to make your vision for the future a reality. Our time on this planet is so brief. We must not waste even a minute. I wish you Godspeed on your quest to bend the moral arc of the universe toward justice.

## CHAPTER 1

# Purpose is the Heart of Progress

*"Do not go where the path may lead.*
*Go instead where there is no path and leave a trail."*
—Ralph Waldo Emerson

I awoke from less than five hours of restless sleep, rolled over, and looked at my phone. *The New York Times* alert was unmistakable:

> *Republican presidential nominee Donald J. Trump has been elected the 45th president of the United States.*

I put the phone back on the nightstand and stared at the ceiling.

*Do I have it in me to remove myself from this bed?* I wondered.

Everything felt electric and unreal, as though one spark of static electricity could make the world explode. Perhaps

I would wake momentarily and discover this was all a dream. I sat up and swung my legs out of bed. I looked again at the news alert, replaced the phone, and shook my head. I closed my eyes. There, on the carpet beside my bed, my knees dropped out from under me; I collapsed as though in slow motion into the fetal position and cried. It was November 9, 2016.

Days earlier I had written an impromptu poem called "The Last Mile," a desperate salvo to my team of organizers and volunteers to give everything they could to the cause.

"These are the moments that test our mettle, our courage, our commitment," I wrote.

"Give today what you do not have left and it shall be returned to you a hundred-fold."

Ha. Ha-ha.

I couldn't decide whether to laugh or cry from the cruel irony of it. I couldn't imagine that we had worked so hard, only to lose. How was it possible for so many millions of human hours of effort to add up to defeat?

The tears were not those of the gut-wrenching cry I knew was coming. These were overflow tears, the raw excretion of exhaustion and disbelief. Lying on the floor in the fetal position, my forehead pushing into the strangely pleasant abrasion of the rug, I thought for a moment about turning off my phone and crawling back into bed. No one would dare look for me, much less try to extricate me from forced hibernation. Perhaps I could pretend for a few more hours—days?—that the unthinkable had not happened. But no.

After several minutes that seemed to stretch into eternity, I summoned the strength to lift my forehead from the floor, and got to my feet. I walked down the stairs and into the kitchen and got out a frying pan and eggs, just as I had done every morning for the past seventy days. My father sat at the kitchen table, scanning the newspaper, awaiting my arrival.

In the midst of working eighty-hour weeks, I had been blessed to spend the months working on the campaign living at home with my dad, something I had not done since I was four years old. Though the hours I had spent at home were limited, he had watched the whole saga unfold. He had seen it all, from my early, quaint insistence in August that Donald Trump *could* win and *must* be stopped, to the horrifying days that followed James Comey's red-herring email announcement. He rose from the kitchen table and came toward me with his arms open, inviting a hug. "Come here, sweetie," he said. "I'm so sorry." I let my father's warm embrace take me in. How lucky I was to wake up to the strong, calming presence of a parent who had witnessed my life up to this moment and who would surely be there to observe the lessons I learned in the process.

*What was this horrible reckoning meant to teach us?* I wondered silently to myself. *How can I turn this drowning feeling of despair into a rally cry for future victory?*

After a few moments, I released my arms and stepped back, meeting my father's eyes with a tight smile. He put his hands on his hips. "You know," he said, shaking his head, "sometimes you only learn when you lose." Those seven words, so hard to hear in that moment, became my mantra for the months that followed.

I realized then that no amount of analysis, polling, or pavement pounding guarantees a win. The functional mechanics of a campaign are a necessary—but insufficient—foundation for victory. What were we missing?

Though not a political retrospective, in many ways this book is my answer to this question. It is not a campaign "insider's" take on "what went wrong"—I was, after all, just a field organizer, quite low on the totem pole. In this book, I strive to capture lessons I have learned throughout my career that I believe can help us progress toward a new form of activation and engagement for both political and social causes.

Facing a setback like the one the Democratic Party suffered in 2016, I find myself balancing the polarity of despair and hope. The failure of party leaders to support a different approach to politics in America leaves me forlorn, while at the same time the success of new movements and young, progressive candidates fills me with hope. Building toward a new, ambitious future sometimes means grieving our past (and present) failures, all the while learning from the mistakes of our lived experience. This belief is at the foundation of this book and informs the way I work with my clients, too. The Heptagon Method is the result of my attempt to systematize what I've learned throughout my life and career, including the hard lessons from the 2016 campaign. As much as I may wring my hands in despair on any given day, I believe deeply in the promise of positive change. As you read, I hope that you can apply these lessons to advance your personal vision for change in the world, whatever that vision may be.

## The Heptagon Method

The Heptagon Method is a seven-step framework designed to help mission-driven organizations develop brands that inspire action. For the purposes of this book, I take the term "mission-driven" to refer to organizations guided by purpose, principally nonprofits, but also social enterprises, educational institutions, and other community service organizations, as well as businesses and political campaigns.

In my work with such organizations, I have seen their leaders fall prey to three common mistakes that get in the way of them achieving their goals. First, they converge too soon, rushing to action, launching an ambitious fundraising campaign before they have laid a clear pathway of engagement. When such efforts do not deliver the desired result, they believe the failure was with the campaign, whereas very often it was in the failure to lay the appropriate groundwork for success. Second, many organizations approach marketing and communications haphazardly, launching new tools and tactics as circumstances arise. They lack a framework to guide effective strategy. Lastly, many organizations often *assume* that their supporters share the same core understanding of mission, vision, and values, rather than taking the time to validate their shared conviction.

The Heptagon Method provides a seven-step framework that addresses each of these concerns. By clearly defining the steps required to build and amplify a successful brand, this approach instructs a sequence of actions that can mitigate the house-on-fire ad hoc energy that too easily overtakes so many organizations in their efforts to communicate. Most importantly, the method emphasizes the importance of belief as a starting place for action. Here are the seven steps:

1. Ideology
2. Identity
3. Message
4. Story
5. Experience
6. Community
7. Action

The Heptagon Method summarized in this book is my attempt to inspire you to see your ability to reimagine how you advance your cause in the face of seeming constraints. Believing in a big, bold, ambitious idea is often the hardest part. If you believe things should be different—whatever *things* might be, odds are, with a clear supportive structure and defined underlying beliefs, you can inspire others to join you in advancing your vision for change.

## A Little Bit About Me

While recent political events inspired me to write this book, the 2016 election was only the mirror offering me the chance to reflect on my own experience. As I reflected, I began to see how my beliefs could shape the reality of others. The second-wave feminists' rally cry, "The personal is political," seems an appropriate slogan for our journey together. To get us started, here is a bit about me:

The only child of divorced parents, I spent much of my childhood entertaining myself. Starting at age five, I attended a Waldorf school, which explicitly forbids electronic media. This prohibition meant I was typically imagining something. Photos of my childhood depict a perpetual state of costume change, using props and makeup to support the creation of new characters, not just on Halloween. It would be another few decades before I would learn what being a producer actually meant, but as early as age five, I saw life as a production.

While these early productions were uneven at best, over the course of my life and career, I've realized how profoundly these early experiences shaped my view of the world. Making change in the world is hard: demanding the ability to summon conviction and determination; to imagine realities that do not yet exist; to try and fail; and try again.

The four big lessons that follow have shaped my life and career, and also inform this approach.

**1. The practice of making the impossible feasible starts with the unwavering determination to do something that scares the shit out of you.**

"ONE. TWO. THREE."

The three syllables echoed around me as I stared down past my toes into the deep aquamarine waters of the diving well. I swallowed, closed my eyes, and jumped.

I felt the air whiz past me for far longer than felt normal. I broke the water's surface, plunging several feet to the bottom of the diving well, and began struggling toward the surface. I pushed myself upward, treading water, looking longingly at the coaching chair.

With chlorine water streaming out of my hair and down my face, I met the eyes of a small, gaunt Chinese woman. Her furrowed brow and tight lips matched her dark look of disappointment. She shook her head, tightly.

"You no jump on three," she said. "You go again."

In his youth, my father was a competitive swimmer and diver at his local town pool, and he wanted to indoctrinate me into the tradition. He lived nearby the Kennedy Shriver Aquatic Center in Bethesda, MD, home to the US Olympic Swimming and Diving teams. The auspicious and impressive training facility offered an eight-lane Olympic-length pool adjoined by a diving area that included two pairs of one-meter and three-meter springboards, as well as five-, seven-, and ten-meter platforms that towered over the twenty-foot-deep diving well. A water slide descended from the ten-meter platform, enticing fearful young would-be divers to make the climb and inspect the distance, while still offering a safer route of escape.

The summer I was eight, my father enrolled me in a two-week diving camp, geared toward seven- to nine-year-old kids. Our head coach, Hwa, a Chinese Olympian who had made a name for herself during the Olympics of the 1980s, had the intensity you might expect. She demanded extraordinary discipline and commitment from her young charges. Always crystal clear on her expectations of performance, Hwa suffered no fools and took nonsense from no one.

At the end of the first week of camp, she ordered us up to the five-meter platform, where each diver was instructed to jump on the count of three. I moved to the back of the group, angling to be one of the last to make the jump. I was not afraid of heights as much as I was terrified of finding out exactly what it would feel like to hit the water from such a height. *Would it hurt?* I wondered. *Will I injure myself by accident?* Such was my state when my turn came, and I stepped to the edge of the platform. What I failed to realize was the importance of the count.

"You no jump on three. You go again."

I swam to the edge of the pool, laddered up, and took the stairs to the five-meter platform. All of the other kids had successfully completed their jumps on three and were drying off or headed home. I walked out to the edge of the platform to await the count. Once again, the three syllables echoed out across the expanse, as I tried to steel myself. Again, I failed, finally summoning the courage to hurl myself over the edge, the sixteen feet of airspace feeling like an endless time-space continuum. Again, I surfaced, knowing what I would hear next.

"Again," Hwa said, shaking her head.

I padded around the edge of the pool, feeling like a failure, but also dreading the spectacle of failing to jump on the count, yet again. Another coach, Mike, was sitting near the three-meter board, providing after-hours coaching to a few older divers. I had started up the stairs to the five-meter platform, passing the three-meter boards on my right, when I had an idea.

"Hey, Coach Mike," I called. He turned around and smiled. I smiled back. "Can I go home?" I asked sheepishly.

He turned around to look at the clock on the other side of the pool. "Sure, honey! It's after six. You're all done for the day."

Relieved to have avoided another baleful summons, I walked back down the stairs and out across the pool bridge, hoping I would be far enough away to be out of sight from Hwa. Virtually tiptoeing in plain view through the very center of the facility, I made it about twenty feet before Hwa's voice echoed across the pool.

"ALICIA!" she yelled. "Where you go?"

I turned around, knowing I was doomed. "Um, Coach Mike said I could go home?" I said.

"You no jump on three!" Hwa yelled. "You go again."

The remaining divers and parents in the pool area had fallen silent at this point, watching a hard-handed coach demand commitment to performance from an eight-year-old. I turned and slowly walked up the stairs to the five-meter platform, knowing I had no choice in the matter.

If I wanted to go home and sleep in my bed that night, I would have to summon the courage to jump on three. Of course, I had already made the jump twice without dying—my body was practically twitching with adrenaline. I drew myself up, prepared to begin to jump on "two."

"ONE, TWO, THREE," the count rang out, again.

I jumped with determination into the air, keeping my body taut, toes pointed. For the first time, I began to relish the surging adrenaline of being airborne. I entered the water with barely a splash. Reemerging above the water's surface, I looked up at Hwa. A faint smile spread across her face. She nodded, and turned away, without saying a word.

By the end of the second week, I was diving backward off the three-meter platform with gusto, Hwa's lesson of the count at that point a distant memory. Years later, I would come to appreciate the extraordinary privilege of having gained that tough resilience so early in my life, and how much it shaped my personality and achievements going forward. "It's only fun if you're not sure it's going to work"; my oft-quoted motto echoes the attitude of an eight-year-old who learned to hurl herself off a sixteen-foot platform, on command.

If you are lucky, life will open doors that offer you the chance to do something terrifying. Something so crazy, you may question your sanity in your willingness to risk everything to do it. Lurking at the bottom of this pit of questions and uncertainty is fear, fear that you are not enough, fear that you will fail. Fear is the force of nature that gives you permission to put your head down, keep quiet, and make yourself small. Yet change does not begin with smallness. It starts with a big, ambitious idea, and a recognition that, though it may seem impossible, you are willing to stake your most precious gift—your time here on Planet Earth—to see it realized.

Both Henry Ford and Yoda are right:

> "Whether you think you can, or you think you can't—you're right."
> "Do. Or do not. There is no try."

Such clarity of conviction defines ideology. You have to find the words for the scary-crazy-ridiculous-impossible dream you have for the future. You have to define the beliefs that will guide you on your journey to get there. Impossibility drives progress. As you will learn in Chapter 3, a clear ideology plants the seeds of imagined possibility that can one day grow into an audacious and inspiring future.

Standing frozen in fear will get you nowhere other than exactly where you are. Instead, you have to practice pointing fierce determination at dubious circumstances. Your best work often comes when you accept that there are factors outside your control and things you can only learn from experience. Sometimes the best thing you can do is jump.

## 2. Miserable failure is usually a sound indication you are doing it wrong.

Six years after the jump-on-three lesson, two months into my first year at Miss Hall's School, I found myself in high school physics class, facing a new kind of personal failure, my first real test score. In red ballpoint pen, at the top of the page bore the ugly truth: 59%.

I had the first nine years of my schooling in Waldorf education, which encourages children to sing, dance, and play well into middle school. Academic subjects are taught mainly through interactive activities rather than traditional book learning. The 59 percent was a stark reminder those years were behind me. My teacher might as well have written FAILURE.

I sat at the front of the class, grateful that I couldn't see the grades of any of the students behind me. I stared down at the page, feeling the tears begin to tickle the backs of my eyes. *Do not cry,* I thought to myself. *You will not cry right now. Not here. Not now.*

My physics teacher was kind enough to deliver bad news at the end of class. I managed to escape the room and run to my academic advisor's office, before collapsing into tears. "I'm a faaa-a-a-a-aaaaaaiiilure!" I wailed, throwing myself onto her office sofa and shoving my face into a couch pillow. The grim determination of the five-meter jump was, at this moment, a distant memory. My advisor was familiar with the gentler approach of Waldorf education. She smiled, sat down beside me, and folded me into a hug.

"Awww honey," she said, chuckling softly to herself. "You're going to be fine."

She waited until I had resumed breathing normally before she started to ask more probing questions. "So, how did you study for the test?" she asked.

I looked at her quizzically. *Study?*

She giggled. "How do you think you're supposed to pass physics, if you don't prepare for your tests?" she asked.

I was dumbfounded. Ridiculous as it sounds, I was fourteen years old and had never had to study for a test before. I didn't know how.

Together, we reviewed my syllabus and made a schedule of when I would check in with her on my progress preparing for my next test. For the next six weeks, she drilled me on the fine print of whatever I had learned that week, to ensure I was both paying attention in class and putting the work in during my homework assignments to understand the concepts.

When I sat down to take the next test, I was ready. I pulled out a pen, looked down at the paper, and got to work. I fail to recall the second test score as vividly as the first, but it was well above passing. I scored well above 90 percent on each test thereafter to end the year with an A-minus.

Beyond the equations for centripetal force, momentum, and gravity, the biggest lesson I learned that year was how important it is to put in the work. It is tempting to show up, wing it, and hope for the best. It is much harder to hunker down, get disciplined, and execute a plan of attack.

Sometimes extraordinary failure is the only thing strong enough to make you reconsider your approach. Confirmation bias often gets in the way of organizations achieving their goals, and can be exceptionally hard to escape and overcome. Some circumstances demand the courage for you to take the leap off the five-meter platform. Others require the grit and determination to commit yourself to a new way forward. It is not a matter of hardening your commitment, but of thinking differently about how to approach the problem at hand.

In Chapter 4, you will read a great deal about PYXERA Global, an organization that made a monumental decision to change its identity twenty years after its founding. The decision to rebrand is one of the most difficult an organization will face. The tradeoffs seem huge, the future uncertain. "If you do what you've always done, you get what you've always gotten." Doing what you have always done comes naturally. Doing something new can be both terrifying and challenging. Fear is often the biggest obstacle to your ability to reimagine what is possible. For legacy organizations, surrendering old habits and established brand equity, and stepping into an unknown future, can be nothing short of terrifying. Yet, change is inevitable. It is just a question of whether the disruption of change drives you, or whether you drive change. With the bright light of your ideological conviction to guide you, the next right action becomes clear, giving you the courage to defy the status quo.

### 3. The conviction of a higher purpose shines the brightest light.

Near the end of my junior year of high school, I faced another proverbial five-meter jump. During the preceding three years, I had become friends with two girls who were on a mission to rule the school in true *Mean Girls* fashion. While I had actively participated in student council, I had also acquiesced to their whims, at times giving up my leadership roles at their insistence that they were more deserving or qualified. Senior year, their plan for school domination would finally be realized: one would become student-body president; the other, president of the senior class. Because of the nature of our relationship, I had never considered running, until one day when I ran into Al, the head security guard.

Al had been a warden of the school for decades. Miss Hall's was then home to more than 150 girls, and Al could always be found walking the halls, keeping everyone safe. Adored by every student at the school, he was a living institution.

I walked into the dining hall to get a glass of water and found Al refilling his coffee cup.

"How ya doin', Alicia?" Al asked, baffling me with his ability to remember everyone's name.

"I'm okay," I said. "How are you?"

Al sipped gently at his cup of coffee.

"Oh, you know. The usual," he said, offering me a gentle smile.

I smiled back, filling my water glass.

"Hey, are you thinking of running for student-council president?" he asked, jovially.

I took a long sip, trying not to choke as I searched for a reply.

"Uh no, I don't think so!" I said cheerily. "I guess I was thinking of applying for proctor or something," referring to the seniors selected to serve as dorm supervisors for the younger students.

"That's a shame. The boys and I bet on it every year," he said, the "boys" referring to the team of eight or so security guards and maintenance men who served the school in a variety of capacities. "I put my money on you," he said, giving me a long, unwavering look.

Al took another sip of his coffee. "You know, I've never been wrong." He smiled, his eyes twinkling.

I stood, dumbfounded. "Wow," I said, grasping for words, a strange tingling sensation rising in the pit of my stomach. "Uh, I guess I'll think about it," I said shakily, unsure of how to respond.

Another moment of silence passed as we both finished our drinks and returned our cups to the dishwashing window. We walked together out of the dining hall.

"See ya later," I said, as I turned to walk up the stairs to my room.

Of course, I had thought of the possibility of running for a school leadership position. I had spent the last three years actively involved in student government, team sports, and theatre. I was well-regarded by most of my peers. My decision to attend boarding school—especially an all-girls school—had been a transformative one. I had been deeply inspired by the seniors who had led the school during my first and sophomore years, and I relished the idea of being able to give back to the school and shape the experience of the younger girls who would follow me. In the quiet of my room, where no one could see (or judge) me, I had thought about running for a school leadership position much the same way I had imagined kissing Matt Damon. Just because I could *envision* it did not mean it was actually *possible*. Right? I had taken friends' future leadership for granted, afraid that any aspiration on my part might be interpreted as a challenge. It was strange that someone like Al saw my potential more clearly than I.

The next day I visited my freshman-year physics teacher, who also happened to be the advisor of my would-be opponent, to seek her counsel on running for school president.

"Oh, they'll make your life a living hell," she said, simply. "But there's no question you would make a great president."

Once again, I went back to my room, unsure of what to do. Should I submit myself to the public reputation assassination I knew the decision to run would precipitate? Or forgo the chance to play a significant role in shaping the school's culture and future?

A few days later, the school held a meeting where students who intended to run for school and class positions would indicate their intention by signing up on a public list. By then, I had made up my mind. I sat toward the front of the room and was one of the first to put my name on the list. When it reached my "friends" in the back of the room, audible exclamations of "You've gotta be kidding me!" and "No way!" echoed through the auditorium. I gritted my teeth and smiled tightly. No turning back now. One, two, three: jump.

The next six weeks were pure hell. This time, it was not the frigid water of the diving well that greeted me on the way down, but the nefarious manipulation of adolescent girls. The Mean Girls lived up to their reputation, spreading the worst kinds of rumors about me, based on our delinquent behavior during the early years of our friendship. While each day felt like a trial, once I had made the decision, I would not back down. I would not let their whispered insults intimidate me. I knew that I was running for the right reasons. I ignored the passive-aggressive ridicule and instead focused on preparing the vision I would deliver in my speech to the student body.

On the night of the election, each candidate would give a speech to the convened student body, which was followed by a paper-ballot vote, the results announced forty-eight hours later. The head of school at the time, who has become a lifelong mentor and friend, later told me it was the only student council race in her sixteen-year tenure where she truly did not know who would prevail.

I spoke second, my remarks carefully planned and tirelessly rehearsed. After the idealistic campaign promises I was unlikely to deliver (namely internet in the dorms, in the nascent internet age of 2003), I got to the heart of the matter.

"I know that the student body has been divided by this election," I said. "I believe in collaborative governance, and I pledge to work with whoever wins to move our community forward in the year ahead."

While the tribulations of high school pale in comparison to the trials of adulthood, that moment was for me a reckoning, and a grueling reinforcement of the lesson Hwa had taught me ten years earlier. There on that stage in front of 150 adolescent girls, I came to appreciate the importance of vision and voice. While I ultimately won the election, my victory was by no means certain. I learned how important it is for leaders to not only demonstrate the resilience and resolve to attempt the impossible, but also to demonstrate the insight and perspective to explain why. The stories we tell shape the contours of experience and expectation. Our promise for tomorrow seeds the hope that grows in each of us, if we can muster the courage to let it take root. Purpose is the world's brightest light, and the conviction to connect rather than divide shines even brighter.

As a leader, it is your responsibility to champion the purpose you seek to serve, to empower others to join your movement. Marketers often anchor messaging in customer preferences, trying to find the angle that best motivates a given audience to care. In Chapter 5, you will see how constituent insight can determine how you position your brand. The foundation of your message to your constituents, however, should always be grounded in your core ideology and beliefs. By putting purpose at the heart of how you communicate about your work, you position yourself as a beacon of authenticity and hope. By expressing the vision that others do not yet see, you offer them the inspiration that will allow them to follow.

## 4. You must imagine what might seem impossible to make it real.

The pedagogy of Waldorf education forbids electronic media and plastic toys, so that mostly left my friends and me to fill our time with imaginative play. We spent long hours in the woods, hunting gnomes and fairies, warding off trolls. An iconic home video portrays my best friend Stephanie and me enacting a skit we called the Lord and the Elf. I, the Lord, issued daunting commands that Stephanie, the Elf, comically scrambled to obey. Will Ferrell would probably agree, we were ahead of our time. My early childhood dramatic inclinations gave way to annual Waldorf school productions focused on a theme from the year's curriculum, and my penchant for cross-gender impersonation followed me to high school. As a student at an all-girls boarding school, male actors were in short supply. While boys from the local high school or faculty spouses played starring roles, like Nathan Detroit in *Guys and Dolls*, and Tevye in *Fiddler on the Roof*, many girls donned ties and mustaches to fill out the cast.

Miss Hall's put on two annual productions—a straight play in the fall and a musical in the spring. My senior year, the theatre director announced the fall play in the first week of school: *Harvey*, a choice many considered strange for an all-girls school. The play chronicles the life of Elwood Dowd, an elderly bachelor who befriends a giant rabbit, named Harvey. The problem? Elwood is the only person who can see Harvey. The play chronicles the various interventions his family and others undertake to deal with his apparent insanity.

The director cast me as Elwood. I had become practiced at playing men in at least three other productions, so I was unfazed by the male role. I was much more preoccupied with the substantial challenge of bringing to life an imaginary rabbit on stage. The play includes many conversations between Elwood and Harvey, all of which are heard by the audience from only one side. Curious indeed. Much of the comedy depends on Elwood's ability to show the audience what Harvey is doing, or saying, while the other characters remain oblivious. Elwood's empathy and affection for Harvey bring the invisible rabbit to life for the audience.

In a sense, this play demanded that I inhabit two characters at once, one visible, the other seen only in the viewer's imagination. It was a formative moment in my understanding of the power of belief to shape the experience of others. Alone on stage, deep in conversation with a six-foot-tall (imaginary) rabbit, I learned how to project characters outside of myself, to help people come to believe in a fiction that at some unforeseen future moment might suddenly be all too real. I also realized that the subtle details of a moment in time can immediately transform someone's core beliefs.

Clear ideology, identity, and message provide a strategic foundation from which to launch a movement, but ideas will not amplify themselves. Humans are inherently narrative creatures. We make sense of our past, present, and future in stories. As you will read in Chapter 6, our brains are optimized to process information delivered in narrative form. Our minds mirror another person's experience by simply hearing their story told. The best way to motivate your audience with your message is to embed it in stories. Use experiences of those whose lives you seek to change to inspire others to support your cause.

The twenty-first-century multimedia landscape offers two clear paths by which you can amplify stories. The first is through online and analog content—blog posts, photographs, videos, slideshows, magazine features, and billboard ads. An ever-multiplying array of promotional tools are at your fingertips, and it is critical to offer your audience windows into your work by way of the stories you share. Chapter 6 provides a deep dive into stories and how to tell them for maximum impact. It is important to choose these stories carefully, recognizing that our stories of the present quickly become our history. Of whom, by whom, and how you share your stories of impact are choices that can empower and inspire your audience.

The second promotional path is events, shared experiences that change our hearts and minds, something you'll read more about in Chapter 7. Communally witnessing stories told live, whether through a play, movie, or keynote address, offers both the inspiration of narration and the chance to see beyond ourselves to the collective to which we belong. If a producer is doing it right, I and others enter a theatre as *individuals*, alone—and afterward, we leave as *us*, transformed by the imaginative moments we have shared. The audience shapes its own experience, too. One man with a particularly audible laugh can enrich everyone's merriment, heightening the energy of the experience for the performers and the audience alike. One person's story can help someone envision the broader possibility of radical change at the heart of your ideology. Capturing this magic is both an art and a science. It demands placing stories and human experience at the center of your strategy and building out from there, all the while keeping the vision of the goal you are working toward front and center for everyone.

My goal in writing this book is to bring to life the nuance of the Heptagon Method using these and other experiences. My broader, more audacious goal is to strengthen your ability to reimagine what is possible and to make real what once seemed inconceivable. I hope that this framework will help you avoid the pitfalls of confirmation bias, false urgency, and presumed unity. It should also inspire you to leverage ideological clarity and storytelling to achieve greater impact. Through a combination of psychology, sociology, social science, and personal experience, I have tried to document the sequence of actions that create a pathway for change. At the core of this approach is a fierce focus on the human experience, a commitment to question everything and answer honestly, a conviction to understand what propels us forward and what holds us back. I hope you, like me, will see the enormous opportunity that awaits us when we decide to become champions of higher purpose. I hope this book will provide you with the tools you need to join me as a champion for mission-driven brands that have the power to spark movements that can enhance the world.

## CHAPTER 2

# The Magic Behind the Heptagon Method

*"You never change things by fighting the existing reality.
To change something, build a new model that makes the
existing model obsolete."*
–R. Buckminster Fuller

For decades, certain people of power and privilege in America have successfully organized against justice—to increase segregation and gun ownership, and diminish economic equity within a culture of racialized fear. Many men have persistently exerted their will against women in acts of both subtle and explicit violence, and have depended on their privilege to protect them from prosecution. This book is not about the history and legacy of these threats. In some sense, it presumes a shared understanding of the challenges facing human society, which I believe are especially stark in the United States. This book begins with the baseline assumption that each of us is working on some aspect of a patchwork quilt of change from our own unique niche of understanding and experience. The world has problems that need fixing. This book seeks to answer the question: *What do we do now?* This chapter provides a high-level overview of the method which underlies this book, briefly explaining how each of the seven steps in the Heptagon Method can help you inspire and engage your allies for greater impact.

Change begins with a shared understanding that has the potential to become a movement. If you are reading this book, you most likely have a movement you would like to start. You have an idea that could change everything. You want everyone to know it. To feel it. To see it. To hear it. To believe it, and to believe *in* it.

Movements often seem to start by accident, at a moment's notice. In 2018, the March for Our Lives took the American people by storm, beginning with the crack of an assault rifle in a Parkland, Florida high school and growing nationwide. The Kony 2012 campaign, which highlighted a documentary film about Invisible Children Inc. and the Lord's Resistance Army (LRA) gained international notoriety overnight.[2] In 2010, the self-immolation of a Tunisian fruit seller drew millions of Arabs into the streets in revolutionary protest in more than thirteen Middle Eastern countries, the start of what we now know as the Arab Spring.[3] The Freedom Riders of 1961 sparked a battle for civil rights in America that catalyzed the passage of unprecedented desegregation legislation.[4] Mahatma Gandhi's conviction to resist the British Empire's tax on salt inspired millions of Indians to join the fight for independence.[5]

History suggests that these movements mobilized in minutes, by coincidence, when in reality they were often preceded by a lifetime of endurance by a few hardworking people. Their audacious will to fight for something bigger than themselves set the stage for catalytic action. Often, the movements that seem to gain popular prominence in the blink of an eye were actually nurtured and stewarded for years—even decades—before the change went mainstream. Years of careful attention and curation paid off at the moment when the catalyst finally landed. This is the real magic: movements often do not arise extemporaneously, but rather through the sustained and coordinated efforts of a dedicated few.

The Kony 2012 campaign built on the diligent work of documentary filmmakers who risked their lives to show the atrocities of the LRA to those with the power to do something about it. The Arab Spring started with Mohamed Bouazizi's fearless act of despair, which exposed the hopelessness felt by millions of young Arabs who took to the streets. The Freedom Riders were inspired by activists who similarly but unsuccessfully challenged a Supreme Court ruling fourteen years before. Gandhi's successful civil disobedience grew out of his efforts to defend the rights of Indians in pre-Apartheid South Africa decades earlier. The March for Our Lives arguably began in 2014, when Mayors Against Illegal Guns and Moms Demand Action for Gun Sense in America formed Everytown for Gun Safety, which provided crucial organizational support for the 2018 march. [6]

History has demonstrated again and again that there is no such thing as instant success—only instant recognition. Often, movements begin by trial and error, the slow, leaden crawl of learning by doing, mostly from repeated mistakes. Yet movements need not result from happenstance and luck alone. Today, those who seek to plant the seeds of change need look no further than this book for a framework of positive movement-making.[7] I have woven together the stories of my own experiences to exemplify the ways many organizations have built brands that spark lasting impact.

It is not enough for us to protest oppression and wrongdoing. Objection and resistance are insufficient to deliver the future we all want. We have to know what we stand *for*, not just what we are against. At our core, most of us could say we stand for justice. Unpack that just a little, however, and you will likely find a great many assumptions baked into exactly what "justice" means. What it means to me and what it means to you might be radically different. We must do the work to define and understand the core ideas that drive us to mobilize others to engage for change.

## It All Starts with Ideology

First, make explicit the core ideology that is driving your movement. A word often associated with politics or religion, "ideology" is easily misinterpreted to imply extremism or hardened thinking, but its denoted definition is almost philosophical:

> *ideology [ahy-dee-ol-uh-jee]:*
> *1: visionary theorizing*
> *2: a: a systematic body of concepts especially about human life or culture*
> *b: a manner or the content of thinking characteristic of an individual, group, or culture*
> *c: the integrated assertions, theories, and aims that constitute a sociopolitical program*[8]

Owning an ideology may seem a radical aim for a fledgling endeavor, but it is necessary to inspire action. A movement begins with an idea that represents a collection of deeply held beliefs which, taken together, will drive a desired result.

The summer after I graduated from high school, I got a job as a door-to-door canvasser for the Human Rights Campaign. That summer, I knocked on hundreds of doors across the greater DC metro area, raising money for gender equity and human rights. In the process, I learned how a powerful ideology like that of the HRC can mobilize millions to take action for a cause they endorse. Fast forward twelve years to 2016, when I spent three months working as a field organizer for the Florida Democratic Party on behalf of the Hillary Clinton campaign. In Florida, I learned that the absence of ideology leaves little more than empty talking points that lack the motivating force required to drive momentum and change. People take action on issues they feel passionately about, so ask yourself: *How does my ideology spark passion and commitment? How does it make people feel?* Take the time to clarify your purpose. Define your vision, mission, and values. By making your ideology explicit, you allow others to understand and engage with it.

Chapter 3 explores the contrasting examples of the Human Rights Campaign and the 2016 presidential campaign in greater depth to demonstrate how the presence and absence of ideology can define the energy and success of a movement. By beginning with ideology, the Heptagon Method ensures that your community of advocates can understand your deepest conviction and that the bright light of purpose shines from the heart of your brand. Such clarity of conviction is necessary to inspire a movement for change.

## From Ideology Define Identity

Share an idea with enough people enough times and suddenly the idea gains independence from its source. The idea develops a life of its own. Quickly it gains a short-hand, a referential name that when mentioned by those in the know, conveys meaning: Democrat, Republican, Catholic, Save the Children, Feed the Future, charity: Water, Budweiser, Coca-Cola, Nike, TOMS. Before you know it, and whether you like it or not, that ideology turns into a brand.

Branding has been around for millennia, and just not in the twenty-first-century sense of the term. The word "brand," which we use interchangeably today to mean "company," "logo," and "corporate identity," has its origin in livestock. The concept began with a big piece of metal, a blazing fire, and a need to differentiate animals within the herd. From the time of the Ancient Egyptians to the present day, people have used branding—the application of burning hot metal to an animal's hide—as a marker of ownership and quality. The tiny visual symbol indicating an animal's ownership or origin determined its price. Similarly, the coat of arms of European legions were also brands. A simple, clear marking, emblazoned on shields, armor, and banners, provided a forward-facing differentiator between clans and factions throughout Europe and Asia.

Before I joined the Clinton campaign in Florida, I spent four years working for an international development nonprofit in Washington, DC. Twenty-three years after the organization's founding, they decided to rebrand, and I was hired to coordinate that process. Once we hired a creative agency and defined our ideology, we began the painstaking process of selecting a new name.

We learned that brand names are either explicit or evocative. In the twentieth century, explicit brands, like IBM (International Business Machines), AT&T (American Telephone and Telegraph), EY (Ernst & Young), and PwC (PricewaterhouseCoopers), were common. In that era, brands were often chosen to describe the product the company produced, the service it provided, or for the name of its founder. Such explicit brands, while once mainstream, are less common in newer brands. Even IBM, AT&T, EY, and PwC have come to rely on their acronyms, rather than their explicit brand names. Evocative names are helpful for brands with broad and complex portfolios of work. FedEx, Lego, and Google are all examples of evocative brands. Ultimately, we chose an evocative brand for its simplicity and flexibility to accommodate the organization's evolution over time.

Next, we set out to visualize the brand's ideology with a new logo, an inspiring representation of a brand's underlying purpose. Because of how our brains work, a brand's mark expresses its ideology in a dramatically different way. The left side of our brain is responsible for structured thought—reading words, crunching numbers, understanding logic. The right side of our brain is responsible for creativity and imagination. The locus of subtlety and intuition, the right brain is also the part of the brain that sees and interprets the meaning of images.

Ideally, a brand's name provides an explicit message to the listener's left brain, while the brand's logo sparks the imagination of the viewer's right brain.

A brand's name, logo, colors, and fonts often account for the highest degree of brand exposure, and must be selected with care. As the second step in the Heptagon Method, identity builds on ideology to convert your stated purpose into visual inspiration. To design a new logo, we had to ask: What emotions will someone feel upon seeing this icon? What images will it evoke? What inspiration will it bring to mind? How can we ensure the brand's visual identity will encourage advocates to understand and support our core purpose? Chapter 4 explores this branding process in depth and offers lessons learned from the organization's CEO that can guide those embarking on the process of developing a new brand identity.

## Understand Your Audience, and Clarify Your Message

Once you have defined your ideology and designed your brand identity, you are ready to take your movement to the masses. But to whom? And how?

Simon Sinek is a leading champion of the utility of purpose in shaping how brands communicate. His September 2009 TED talk, "How Great Leaders Inspire Action," and subsequent opus, *Start with Why*, have become guiding lights for those seeking to inspire a connection to their cause. [9]

"There are only two ways to influence human behavior," Sinek says. "You can manipulate it, or you can inspire it." Sinek is quick to point out that manipulation is not always malicious, and it can be an effective way for companies to achieve short-term marketing success. "The danger of manipulations," he writes, "is that they work. And because manipulations work, they have become the norm, practiced by the vast majority of companies and organizations, regardless of size or industry."

Marketing teams often focus on the importance of getting their messaging just right, using the turn of phrase that will best manipulate their customer. Instead of focusing on finding the "right message," purpose-driven brands can use their ideology as a compass, emphasizing different aspects of their purpose to different customer segments.

Defining message requires deciding what you want people to hear and empowering your employees and advocates with the framing they need to amplify your ideology. Getting your message straight means first understanding your audience, and then finding the source of their inspiration. Human-centered design, design thinking, and Lean method (different names for similar practices) are helpful tools for understanding a user's priorities that can help you authentically position your cause to encourage their support.

The Lean Startup Machine weekend boot camp gave me my first hands-on experience with user personas and message validation. Chapter 5 illustrates how to develop a brand message that inspires your audience. The Heptagon Method defines messages based on your ideology, to amplify different aspects of your brand's purpose. Once you clearly understand the concerns of your constituents, you can ensure your message aligns with their personal values to motivate them to take action on behalf of your cause.

## Get Your Story Straight

Stories of human experience help people hear your brand message by exemplifying the power of your ideology to change lives. That means finding storytellers and empowering them to speak on behalf of your movement, to become the voice of your brand. No one enjoys being lectured to about facts and figures. People want to feel relevant, to feel heard. A story you can relate to makes something theoretical feel personal. Once you have established your ideology and key messages, stories provide a mechanism by which to amplify this important information in a memorable way. Amplifying stories of transformation enabled by your movement can create a groundswell of motivated people who raise their hand and say: *Yes, I'm in!*

Stories effectively inspire advocates by triggering mirror neurons, specific neurological receptors that guide how the brain responds to observed actions.[10] When we watch someone perform a task, mirror neurons allow the brain to replicate the feeling the person performing the task experiences.[11] Some researchers believe that mirror neurons enable humans to feel empathy, allowing us to understand the intention behind an action.[12] Hearing a story is similar to observing an action, provoking a mirrored response. The human experience of the storyteller triggers your mirror neurons, inspiring you to empathize with their experience and share their commitment and resolve.

Marshall Ganz, a senior lecturer of public policy at Harvard University, instructs those wishing to harness the power of story to inspire action to use the practice of public narrative.[13] Ganz describes the important relationship between story and purpose. "Narrative allows us to communicate the emotional content of our values," Ganz writes, clarifying that talking *about* values does not have the same effect as *embodying* values within the narrative itself. By emphasizing their most challenging moments of choice and transformation, you can inspire your advocates to believe in their power to create meaningful and lasting change. Ganz specifically defines three different motivational narratives: the Story of Self, the Story of Us, and the Story of Now, which leaders can use to amplify their core purpose. Ganz cautions that causes without a clear story should beware. Such organizations, he warns "Lack an identity, a culture, core values that can be articulated and drawn on to motivate" action.

At the same time, I was stewarding the rebranding described in Chapter 3, I also served as the editor of a social impact magazine, *The New Global Citizen*. Each year we received dozens of submissions from brand leaders and beneficiaries from around the world, which we published to exemplify our own focus on purposeful global engagement. Chapter 6 draws on the example of this publication to explain why stories are fundamental to human memory and motivation. It reveals how the stories of Self, Us, and Now motivate action, and defines the secret of successful stories, which you can use to empower allies within your movement to tell the stories that matter most.

Stories are at once simple and complex, but one thing is certain: organizations have a great deal to gain from telling great stories. Ideally, this includes both positioning an organization's leaders to tell stories of vision and empowering those you serve to share how they have benefitted from service to its mission. The Heptagon Method uses stories to provide a steady drumbeat of motivation, steadily raising the visibility of the ideology to become more prominent and recognized. Stories, in this way, become the most effective way to bring brands to life, and motivates advocates to act.

## Use Experience to Foster Connection

Once your brand has a reputation, it is time to convene your people. Let them see the multitude who have heard the stories and gotten the message, who share your ideology. Now they are ready to engage more deeply and directly. Personal experience is a powerful thing. Surrounded by people who share your conviction can enhance the depth of your own belief, motivating you to act to propel it forward. Suddenly, for hundreds or thousands of people, your brand becomes a priority.

Experiences help shape human awareness and foster greater connection and community among those present. We enter a space as individuals and leave as a group who have all borne witness to a singular moment in time. The Big Apple Circus, a TED event, or a Bruce Springsteen concert are all moments that write themselves into our memory through our own interpretation of what we feel, see, taste, and smell, within a shared period of time and space. Seating arrangements, venue selection, and the type of communication participants receive before, during, and after an event shape their engagement and experience. [14] A simple invitation to attend an event can become the initiation of a deeper level of belonging.

Faith, whether religious or superstitious, is a mysterious thing cultivated by ritual. Francesca Gino and Michael Norton, both professors at Harvard Business School, have studied the use and effects of ritual on human behavior. "People engage in rituals," Gino and Norton claim, "with the intention of achieving a wide set of desired outcomes, from reducing their anxiety to boosting their confidence, alleviating their grief to performing well in a competition—or even making it rain."[15] Evidence has demonstrated that the intention of the ritual has special powers. Gino and Norton point to a number of studies (including their own) conducted between 2010 and 2013, "demonstrating that rituals can have a causal impact on people's thoughts, feelings, and behaviors." Perhaps it is our mirror neurons at work, but there need not be a direct relationship between the ritual and the desired result. According to Gino and Norton, "Performing rituals with the intention of producing a certain result appears to be sufficient for that result to come true."

From my early life experiences onstage, I grew into a producer, first crafting student-run theatre productions like *The Laramie Project* in college, and later in life curating multiday conferences like The Global Engagement Forum and The Unrig the System Summit. The same notions of ritual that have shaped practices of worship for millennia are at work today in the experiences we curate and produce for public consumption. Watching a play on stage, sitting in a theatre surrounded by other moviegoers, or sitting on a crowded lawn listening to live music, we know when to stand, when to clap, when to cheer, and when to sit silently and listen. These are all micro-rituals of experience. Every choice a curator or producer makes, whether it be who speaks from where, or where everyone sits, ripples through the hearts and minds of those present, weaving the gathered masses into an engaged multitude.

Chapter 7 explores the art and science of creating conversion experiences, based on my own experience of producing a variety of events. I explain how the Heptagon Method uses experience to inspire your advocates. Through direct exposure to your storytellers and ideology, you can foster unity and connection that creates a community of champions prepared to advocate for your cause.

---

## The Importance of Community

Individuals who have lived the same experience feel a strong common bond. To spark a movement effectively, you must direct the momentum of a participant's shared experience into the structure of community. Organizations that capitalize on this truth can tap the power of community to transform their brand and accelerate their impact. People want to feel they are a part of something that will endure. They want to feel surrounded by a community of people who share their ideology and conviction to be a part of something bigger than themselves. It is up to you to create a container big enough to hold them, to help those with the commitment to do so to opt in to join your community of allies.

Communities foster connection and shared identity among the converted. Sometimes they form entirely of their own accord. The invention and popularization of Meetup, for example, has made it simple for individuals with shared interests to find one another at a common time and space.[16] Sports fans will find their community at the same bar, or the same stadium, week after week. Alumni of the same alma mater automatically find a common bond with one another, even in unlikely places. Those of the same nationality in another country will likely find an affinity with one another.

I had unwittingly been a part of many such communities for decades before I joined the one that helped me understand how communities catalyze change. In the summer of 2017, I attended the StartingBloc Institute, anticipating a fairly mundane professional development experience. Instead, I found myself surrounded by a highly engaged and socially conscious community of 3,000 other social-impact advocates who were each eager to support one another's dreams.

Authentic communities sometimes seem to emerge by accident when most often they are intentionally cultivated. Extensive research has identified five key components of successful communities: people, purpose, practice, place, and progress. Start with the obvious: the human beings who make up your community. Second, define the purpose, or ideology: the core unifying mandate that motivates people to show up. Third, define what you are doing here: the practice that fosters mutual connection and unity of action. Fourth, these individuals, united in their shared purpose and common practice, demand a place, whether virtual or live, to connect and commune. Lastly, communities thrive on a shared sense of measured progress: the feeling that together you are advancing your cause.

After curating an experience—like a conference, a webcast, or even a conference call—leaders must provide the structure to support a community's ongoing connection to the brand. Live and online group engagement, regular email updates, and published stories help to inspire the community's empathy and commitment. Worn paraphernalia—jerseys, bracelets, rings, and branded clothing—empower community members to show their pride in belonging.

In the days after the 2016 election, an exciting thing happened. A few people sitting around a kitchen table in Washington, DC created a Google Doc they shared on Facebook. Written by DC policy wonks, it provided everyday people with clear instructions on how to lobby their elected representatives effectively. The Indivisible Guide became famous virtually overnight, spurring hundreds of thousands of citizens to take action to protect against a perceived threat to American democracy.

Thanks to the overbearing saturation of the American media, we had all seen the same story unfold for months, and we had all witnessed the same moment of utter loss and unlikely victory. In that moment, progressive Americans were more united than perhaps ever before in recent history. An unnamed, unmarked community had formed virtually overnight. Indivisible threw the fuel on the fire to provoke that community to take action.

Chapter 8 delves into the example of StartingBloc and acroyoga to demonstrate how collectives take shape, and how you can cultivate communities of advocates who share your ideology. The Heptagon Method helps build a bridge from experience, through community, to action. While purpose-driven organizations may not sell over-sized foam cheese-block hats to their advocates, it is possible to harness the same power of ritual and connection to motivate constituents to collaborate and take action, to advance your brand's purpose and increase its impact.

## Inspire Action to Achieve Impact

Once you have created a community, an inner circle of people connected by stories and experience, your community is ready to take action. Call them to arms with love and devotion, and they will ask what they can do for your movement. *Raise money? You bet! Donate money? No problem! Buy products? Just tell me where. Stand in protest? Volunteer?* Allies mobilized by a shared ideology are overwhelmingly powerful. United, they can accomplish anything. Together, they will create a movement of such momentum that it will make your dreams come true. Your advocates will turn your inkling, your tiny idea that once upon a time seemed like a far-off place, into reality.

Compelling communities to take action on behalf of a brand can sometimes feel like hard work, but that usually means a piece of the Heptagon Method is missing. When the foundation is complete, communities are eager to share, give, raise, and volunteer in any way they can. It is up to brands to provide a constructive pathway for activation. A community does not have to be especially large to have a significant impact. According to researchers at Rensselaer Polytechnic Institute, "Once 10% of a population is committed to an idea, it's inevitable that it will eventually become the prevailing opinion of the entire group. The key is to remain committed."[17]

Once you feel a part of something, you want to help move it forward. In order to take action, the community must feel how their efforts connect to progress. People can share a piece of content through social media or buy a product that represents a greater good. With even higher levels of commitment, they may even raise money on behalf of an organization or donate directly to a cause. In Chapter 9, I explore all of the ways that brands can encourage action on behalf of a cause, and how sequencing your calls to action can cultivate an individual's growing commitment over time. The Heptagon Method helps brands work through the first six steps required to reap the rewards of action that can spark movement toward meaningful positive impact.

Movements evolve and brands at different stages of evolution benefit from different kinds of support. Starting a movement to power a fledgling cause means building a new brand. This process is the most straightforward: start with step 1 and work straight through to seven. For established organizations working to launch a new initiative or drive new energy into their existing community, the Heptagon Method can serve as an auditing framework. Evaluating the organization's performance at each step will ensure that a strong foundation exists for action. Sometimes well-established institutions become complacent in their communication and marketing efforts. They may fall prey to the allure of manipulation for short-term gain or take actions that later prove to be unethical. Enough missteps can rupture established trust between a brand and its advocates, resulting in a broken brand. When it comes to healing a broken brand, remedial action is often required to redefine shared ideology and rebuild trust. Chapter 10 reviews in detail cases of new, underperforming, and broken brands to analyze how the Heptagon Method can address each one.

The final chapter revisits the core assumptions ingrained in the method, summarizing the key actions within the seven-step approach and articulating how a systematic approach to brand development can spark action that leads to meaningful social change. You will see how this framework will become a momentum engine, in which actions seed stories that catalyze experiences that, once again, inspire communities to take action.

## CHAPTER 3

# Put Your Mission Where Your Mouth Is

*"If you stand for nothing . . . what'll you fall for?"*
—Lin-Manuel Miranda, *Hamilton*

I was eighteen years old, standing in the middle of a room full of chattering college students knocking on clipboards, asking one another for money. One question kept flashing through my mind.

*Why are you here?*

I had just graduated from high school and had planned to spend the summer living with a friend in Northern Virginia, working as a restaurant hostess. But because I had almost no service-industry experience, no one wanted to train me for the three months I was available to work.

I found alternative employment by way of a sign taped to a telephone pole.

MAKE $4,000–$6,000 THIS SUMMER DEFENDING HUMAN RIGHTS, the poster promised.

Nine little fingers of paper with a name and phone number printed on each one dangled from the bottom. CALL ELAINE, they instructed. One of a dozen fingers of paper had already been torn away. I pulled out my cell phone, typed in the ten numbers, and hit send.

"Fund for Public Interest Research, this is Steve," a male voice proclaimed on the other end of the line.

"Hi, my name is Alicia," I said hesitantly. "I'm calling for Elaine?" (I had yet to learn how to keep the question mark out of the end of my sentences.)

"Hey, Alicia," Steve said. "Thanks for calling! Elaine's not here right now, but maybe I can help. Are you calling about the job?"

Steve invited me almost immediately to stop by their office to interview. The next day, I found myself standing outside a somewhat dilapidated brownstone. I rang the bell and a college-aged staffer greeted me and shepherded me up to the second floor. After filling out an application and answering a few questions about why I was interested in the job, I was scheduled for a shift the next day. Start time: noon. The entire process took less than an hour. I left, mystified by the ease of the whole process, uncertain what exactly I would be doing, but thrilled to finally have a summer job.

The day of my interview the office had been largely empty when I arrived at 3 o'clock, but when I arrived the next day at noon, the place was swarming with humans. On the floor in one room, a group of people sat huddled over maps cut from atlases of the greater DC metro area, yellow highlighters in hand. In another, a group taped documents to clipboards and counted out donation forms. Everything buzzed.

I wandered up to the second floor, looking for a familiar face, and finally identified my interviewer from the previous day. "Hi!" I said, unsure of what to say next. He smiled pleasantly, clearly not recognizing me. "I'm Alicia. You scheduled me for the shift this afternoon?" I said, hesitantly.

"*Oh!* Hey! Alicia, yeah! Great. Glad you're here! I'm Alex, by the way. We're going to get started in a little bit. You can hang out right over there"—he pointed to the largest room on the second floor—"and you can start reviewing this." He handed me a clipboard stacked with information describing the damaging effects of the Federal Marriage Amendment and advocating support for the Human Rights Campaign.

Our job as door-to-door canvassers was to raise money. The clipboard was our only tool to persuade donors to give. Leaning against a wall, I began to examine the laminated sheets of paper attached to the clipboard, wondering about the intended use of each one. Among them was a script, a campaign fact sheet, and a Human Rights Campaign overview. Standing awkwardly at the side of the room, having never before engaged in this strange prelaunch ritual, I stood like a wallflower, waiting to be asked to dance. Soon, a woman I would later learn was a director, spotted me and immediately engaged. "Give me a knock!" she instructed, cheerily, indicating that I should knock on the back of my clipboard to imitate a knock on a door. I stumbled through my first attempt at the script, losing my place and failing to make eye contact. She gave me an easy win, a fake one-time contribution of $50.

"Don't worry," she said with a smile. "It gets easier, the more you do it."

Right she was. Every day that week, I joined more than fifty canvassers who, again and again, drilled the words that would make a difference, absorbing the facts of the proposed amendment, and learning how to motivate the diverse community of the Washington, DC metro area to underwrite the marriage equality campaign.

*Why are you here?*

The answer to this question is the most important truth behind a brand, one which both brand leaders and brand advocates must be able to answer with ease. Whether you are the CEO or a marketing manager, you are a brand leader, which means the buck stops with you when it comes to communicating your purpose. How people engage with your organization and its purpose is your responsibility. You have to know what that purpose is—*why anyone should show up for your cause*—before you can communicate about it. Creating a foundation of purpose for a brand provides a clear and authentic connection with those it seeks to serve. A clear forward-looking conviction provides a promise of a better tomorrow that everyone can support.

According to Simon Sinek, "We trust those with whom we are able to perceive common values or beliefs." A clear statement of belief must extend beyond profit. Financial goals are insufficient to inspire allegiance. You must describe the aspirational future your movement seeks to inspire. "Trust begins to emerge," Sinek says, "when we have the sense that another person or organization is driven by things other than their own self-gain."

Mobilizing your advocates to take action demands clearly understanding the ideology that drives the movement. Often, you feel its presence in a brand without necessarily being able to identify where it comes from or how it got there. At its core, ideology has three parts: vision, mission, and values.

**Vision** defines the aspirational future state the movement seeks to achieve, including the specifics of how it looks. Once an organization has achieved this goal, it must completely reframe its next objective. For many nonprofits, visions are lofty aims unlikely to be reached in our lifetime. But in the near term, the collective intention motivates everyone to keep showing up.

**Mission** describes how your organization will work to achieve its vision. Ideally, a mission statement provides two key benefits to a brand. First, it clarifies what an organization does and does not do. (A think tank that publishes research and analysis, for example, would have a very different mission from a school.) Most importantly, it provides a succinct yet inspiring statement of an organization's core activities.

Many different organizations could share the same vision but work to achieve it in different ways. A shared vision may even allow organizations to become partners or allies. For example, an organization that provides children in Africa with access to nutritious food, inspiring teachers, and social-emotional learning opportunities could state its vision as "improving the future prospects of Africa's children." So, too, could an organization working to provide access to off-grid electricity in Africa.

*The Human Rights Campaign—known widely as HRC—is the leading organization advocating for the equal rights of lesbian, gay, bisexual, transgender, and queer (LGBTQ) individuals. By inspiring and engaging individuals and communities, HRC strives to end discrimination against LGBTQ people and realize a world that achieves fundamental fairness and equality for all.*[18]

HRC prominently displays this mission on its website. The statement seeks to convey aspiration and depth, emphasizing a broad focus on fairness and equality rather than explicitly framing its focus in terms of the organization's advocacy on behalf of the LGBTQ community.

In addition to the mission and vision, high-impact organizations also have explicit values, beliefs that guide how and why they pursue their mission and vision. For nonprofits, mission and vision have always been central to their existence. Yet, as the culture of social impact has expanded, almost every organization has begun to address the same priorities. For many founders and executives, a bold vision of future possibility emerges naturally. A bold vision, however, will not protect a brand from the challenges that can overtake it along the way. Once a company gets big enough and influential enough, that ambitious future vision can fade from view. Companies will trade long-term impact for short-term gain in order to increase their margins. Without values as a guide, a singular pursuit of profit can easily overtake a commitment to a deeper purpose.

An ambitious vision, while awesome and awe-inspiring, is necessary but insufficient to sustain future progress.

Integrating values with vision is the essence of purpose. The aspirational future state you seek is supported and enhanced by the guiding principles you will observe on the journey to get there. The intersecting conviction of values and vision is the essential foundation of ideology. By making the shared values and vision the heart of your organization's work, you create a moral compass that guides every single person working toward the same goals to advance the change you wish to see in the world.

While nonprofits can fall prey to a corporate culture of competition—fear that another's gain is their loss—organizations with clear ideologies need not compete with one another. While there may be overlap in a shared vision and even a similar mission, clarifying the values shared by founders, staff, and stakeholders will often provide sufficient distinction.

Two contrasting experiences help exemplify the important role a clear ideology can play in a movement's success.

## When Short-Term Goals Support Long-Term Impact

In the landmark summer of 2004, HRC's ideology provided a unifying beacon for canvassers and donors alike. In late 2003 and early 2004, Massachusetts and San Francisco legalized marriage for same-sex couples. This local legislation contradicted the federal Defense of Marriage Act, which defined marriage as a union between a man and a woman. Preempting a judicial challenge, President George W. Bush announced his support for a constitutional amendment banning same-sex marriage. In response, HRC mobilized an army of paid canvassers to raise money and garner support in opposition to the amendment.

At the time, the internet relative to its current omnipotence was still in its infancy. Online giving was still in the experimental phase, and few organizations had websites or marketing strategies optimized to receive online donations. As a result, organizations like HRC depended a great deal on canvassing programs to meet their grassroots donation goals. The organization's temporary staff expanded dramatically that summer to meet the campaign's ambitious fundraising targets. Even as canvassers, we clearly understood the organization's core ideology. As a door-to-door canvasser, I had the chance to experience the strength of HRC's ideology firsthand.

From an organizational perspective, a door-to-door canvasser is at the bottom of the pecking order. Seasonal hires without benefits, all of us would be gone in a matter of months. Most members of the team were college students buffing their credentials for future employment in Washington, DC, following graduation. At eighteen, I was still trying to grasp the requirements of my first real job. The canvass was not for the faint of heart. I soon learned that the speedy acceptance I had experienced at first was ultimately contingent on my ability to perform. Every canvasser had a daily quota to meet to remain employed. Many canvassers flamed out quickly because they just were not comfortable asking strangers for money.

Though the core elements remained the same, I soon found myself straying away from the script, tailoring my pitch to whomever I was addressing. "Hi, I'm Alicia! I'm with the Human Rights Campaign. Do you have a few minutes today for marriage equality?" I would ask. Either someone would give the "Go on . . ." nod, or they would shake their head, avert their eyes, and close the door. They either felt called to support the fundamental ideology, or they did not.

Most people in the greater DC metro area were accustomed to being solicited and would graciously open the door, even if they never intended to give a cent. Our canvass focused on the most liberal areas, specifically targeting streets and addresses with known donors. George W. Bush was nearing the end of his first term. Many people were concerned about the state of the nation, and suitably sympathetic toward our efforts to prevent the amendment from going forward. The impending Federal Marriage Amendment made the case more urgent, but the core mission was still of the highest importance. I shared the key tenets of my cause, inviting supporters to help us end discrimination in order to foster a world that could be fair and equal for everyone.

In mid-July, the Federal Marriage Amendment came up for a vote in the Senate and was successfully voted down. All of the doors we had knocked, the dollars we had raised—spent on lobbying, influencing, and increasing visibility—had done their work. Yet, thousands of college students across America still had summer jobs. The work building the community of the converted did not stop simply because we had won this one fight. As canvassers, we reframed, acknowledging the important accomplishment of defeating the bill. Could we count on your support to sustain our successful work of defending equal rights for all?

When I set out that June to find a summer job, I never expected to support a landmark achievement for America's LGBTQ community. The promised summer earnings on the flier were a more significant incentive than the chance to "defend human rights," whatever that meant to my eighteen-year-old brain. While I initially sought the job because of the promised pay, the underlying ideology behind the campaign kept our team motivated and engaged. Our canvassing team did not complain about the hours we worked or the miles we walked. While everyone had both good and bad days meeting the daily quota, canvassers who made it through the first two weeks typically lasted the rest of the summer. We all knew the quota was more than just an arbitrary milestone. It was a benchmark for the future of the movement. While the ideology was rarely what first drew someone to the job, it solidified each person's commitment to the cause,

keeping us coming back day after day to do the work required for long-term success.

## Rebel Without a Cause: A Political Campaign Without Ideological Clarity

While companies and nonprofit organizations often begin
with long-term outcomes in mind, modern political campaigns, by contrast, are spun up quickly and wound down
just as fast. Candidates are focused on gaining the dollars
and votes needed to win in the short term, rather than
establishing a strong and lasting foundation of brand equity and purpose. Twelve years later, I would once again
find myself knocking doors, this time as a field organizer
for the Hillary Clinton campaign. Despite the promised
advantage of twenty-first-century analytics, getting results in the absence of a clear ideology was dramatically
harder and, ultimately, less successful than the Human
Rights Campaign's monumental summer of 2004.

Political campaigns are a lot like the circus. Meant to
capture your imagination while they are in town, seemingly overnight they fold everything up and vanish. In
some ways, the Clinton campaign is an unfair comparison point to an institution as established as the Human
Rights Campaign. While problematic, modern political
campaigns tend to lack trappings of established mission-
driven organizations. Political strategists spend a lot of
time considering what issues will "play well" with voters,

and relatively little time defining a campaign's values and vision. Managers do not hold staffers to established standards of performance, other than meeting their voter registration or door-knocking targets on a weekly basis. Instead of firing someone for underperformance, campaigns "layer" staff to overcome their shortcomings. Yet the similarity of their operational mechanics—mobilizing engagement and commitment through face-to-face conversations—makes for a ready comparison.

In a bygone era, political candidates were merely the latest party standard-bearers, stand-ins for well-known and trusted institutions that were accountable for effective governance while in power. In recent decades, however, public trust in both parties has eroded. In this environment in 2015, Hillary Rodham Clinton embarked on her own brand-building challenge: running for president of the United States.

As a victim of extraordinary character assassination over the course of the previous two decades, Hillary Clinton suffered for the vagueness within her personal brand. Both Senator Bernie Sanders and Donald Trump capitalized on magnifying her perceived character flaws and misbehavior, tiny lies seeded by Fox News and amplified by other media platforms into generally accepted "truths." In some ways, this history perversely shaped the command-and-control culture that dominated the campaign all the way from headquarters in New York down to our field office in Pompano Beach.

In the absence of ideology, all attacks were personal. While Donald Trump ran the news cycle, day in and day out, our chief instruction was dutiful silence. As a field organizer, I was forbidden from speaking publicly about anything other than my prescribed duties. As a result, Hillary Clinton's staunchest supporters—her staff— were effectively unable to share our commitment to the campaign in a way that could positively shape public perception.

Making matters worse, Clinton herself failed to convey a coherent set of values. She offered no authentic and vulnerable stories of the choice moments that had shaped her life. The epitome of the technocratic candidate, she perpetually shielded attention away from herself and onto her platform, extolling the promise of one policy or another for a specific constituency. Aside from her professed focus on "children and families," Hillary Clinton would not explain her own reasons for running for office in authentic or introspective terms. She had no story of self, no story of us, no story of now. She had no choice moments that demonstrated her values and resolve. Indeed, the choice moment that ultimately captured the public's imagination was her mismanagement of her email server and her six-figure, off-the-record speaking engagements at Goldman Sachs. While these "missteps" seemed benign compared to the misbehavior of Donald Trump, the absence of clearly defined values allowed potshots from her opponents to reinforce a perceived lack of integrity.

When I applied to become a field organizer with the Florida Democratic Party in the summer of 2016, I anticipated it would be similar to the work I had done as a paid canvasser for HRC. I understood that "organizing" meant a great deal more than simply knocking on doors and asking for money, but I imagined the same camaraderie and energy, large groups of people wearing I'M WITH HER T-shirts, practicing our pitch, knocking on clipboards, and drilling one another on how to win votes for our candidate.

Unfortunately, I had set myself up for disappointment. I quickly learned that field organizing was rife with acronyms and shorthand. VR, meaning voter registration, described the forms and volunteers assigned to register voters. GOTV, or get out the vote, described the month before Election Day when organizers and volunteers alike would each knock hundreds if not thousands of doors. Turf: the designated geographic area assigned to one canvasser. Call time: the hours between 4 and 8 o'clock during which every organizer needed to call 250 volunteers to persuade them to help register voters or canvass. Flake rate: the percentage of your scheduled volunteers who would fail to show up. Vote plan: when and where a voter would cast a ballot on or before Election Day.

My first day on the job, I was stationed at a folding table in a windowless room and instructed to make 200 phone calls. Instead of knocking on doors and asking for dollars, organizers were expected to make at least 1,750 phone calls per week, calling prospective volunteers to ask them to volunteer their time. Campaign-research mythology suggested that local volunteers were more effective than paid canvassers at motivating voters. Instead of deploying organizers directly to do the work, we were supposed to expand our capacity by recruiting volunteers to do it for us. The list I was calling had just been "re-turfed"—reassigned from someone else—meaning that the best volunteer prospects on my list had already spoken to at least one other organizer. Many were confused and annoyed to receive a call from another stranger. Both they and I would learn to let that go. We were following orders, taking the prescribed actions our leaders promised would elect America's first female president.

Whereas in the summer of 2004 a strong pitch determined the success of your fundraising efforts, the hardest part of organizing volunteers in 2016 was actually getting people to take your call. On average, I would let the phone ring three times before hanging up and dialing the next number; each punched in by hand on my personal cell phone, required for campaign employment. My first day, I made fewer than 80 calls, and by 9 o'clock, I was ready to claw my eyes out. While all-star organizers would get in 280 to 350 calls in three hours on a good day, I would struggle—always—to break 150.

When someone did pick up the phone—once every ten minutes or so—a script instructed us to offer them the chance to attend "an upcoming volunteer event," and ask whether we could pencil them in for a specific time. In September and early October, these "events" were voter registration drives where people with clipboards holding voter registration forms (supplied by me) wandered around public spaces—grocery stores, post offices, libraries, and shopping malls—asking everyone they met if they were registered to vote. Most volunteers expected they were showing up to a party when, in reality, they were showing up to work. A volunteer underwent training on how to register voters legally and successfully. They were then sent forth on a mission to bring back two to five completed forms, which often took anywhere from one to three hours.

This statewide voter registration drive sought to grow the prospective voter pool by a statistically significant margin. The catch was that, as a third-party organization authorized to conduct VR, it was incumbent on us to register any voter, regardless of political interest or affiliation. Often this meant watching silently as someone ticked the REPUBLICAN PARTY box to represent their political affiliation. Sometimes, this meant having the future voter you were helping to register tell you how excited he was to vote for Donald J. Trump.

Once VR ended in October, our focus shifted to GOTV. Florida has two weeks of early voting, so GOTV ran for a full month—a few days to grease the wheels, one week in advance of the start of early voting, a big push during the two weekends of early voting, and then four days of nonstop pavement pounding leading into Election Day, the last chance for voters to cast a ballot.

In 2016, the Florida Coordinated Campaign focused GOTV solely on mobilization which meant only knocking the doors of known Democrats to ensure they had a plan to vote. We were instructed not to waste our time persuading people on the fence to support our candidate. (*Why would we do that, when we could be hitting more doors of likely voters?*) Every person on our list already intended to vote for Hillary Clinton. Our job was to help them make a plan for when and where they would actually do so.

In every instance, we would ask where and when they planned to vote, who they planned to take with them (if anyone), and if they were certain they had the correct form of identification. The conventional wisdom suggested that a face-to-face vote-planning conversation increased a voter's probability of casting a ballot by close to five percent. As a result, every Democrat we spoke to was that much more likely to show up at the polls.

Every day on the job was a grueling ordeal, tirelessly attempting the same five actions, over and over and over again, with diminishing returns. The hours were even longer than promised, the salary a pittance when divided by the hours worked. Like soldiers in the Battle of the Somme, we trudged on day after day, with little understanding of the impact of our actions. "Because HQ says so," was the prevailing answer to any question or criticism that arose from the ranks. Our leadership did not have time for vision and ideology. Overcome by the overwhelming demands of a proverbial house on fire, the campaign dogmatically insisted we maintain the drumbeat of identity politics and true-blue voter mobilization.

## Ideology Guides Tough Choices

Treating the American electorate like an industrial vote-making machine overlooked the core truth of behavioral economics and effective marketing. People vote when their candidate motivates them to believe in an ambitious idea, when they can see a direct connection between their single ballot and the bigger change they wish to see in the world.

When trying to understand how Hillary Clinton lost the election to Donald Trump, a return to Simon Sinek's foundational argument can help elucidate the problem. "Every company, organization or group with the ability to inspire," Sinek says, "starts with a person or a small group of people who were inspired to do something bigger than themselves." Barack Obama's 2008 campaign message of hope and change conveyed a vision of a bigger, better future. Conversely, Clinton's 2016 campaign message, Stronger Together, was strategically designed to exploit identity politics and threatened an unspoken corollary: *weaker alone*. Her technocratic policy expertise, while thoughtful and refined, depended too much on policies and facts to motivate people to care.

If, Sinek warns, an organization "tries too many times to 'seize market opportunities' inconsistent with their WHY over time, their WHY will go fuzzy and their ability to inspire and command loyalty will deteriorate." (Capitalization emphasis, his). Whether these points of deviance were solely perceived or real, the media gained viewership by highlighting Hillary Clinton's inconsistent application of her values. From the handling of her personal email server to her speaker fees for her confidential presentations to Goldman Sachs, these perceived errors of judgment defied the reputation of a candidate committed to governing for the people. The Democratic Party, cast by both Bernie Sanders and Donald Trump as the political outpost of corporate interests, also failed to offer a coherent ideology under which its candidate could stand.

When it comes to adjudicating the 2016 election, most people tend to focus on external effects: James Comey's email announcement; Russian influence on public perception; the broad indifference of Millennial voters; overwhelming public misogyny. No doubt, these factors negatively affected the election outcome. But, without question, the campaign's own internal blind spots defined how the field was organized and ultimately lost. Broward County, the area surrounding Fort Lauderdale, is the bluest county in the state. There, a mobilization focus may have made sense. The mobilization strategy, however, did not stop there but extended across the entire country. [19] Organizers and volunteers alike were not suitably empowered to face a skeptical public with persuasive arguments for why voters should support Hillary Clinton for president.

Most importantly, perhaps, we were given little instruction on how to deal with this rumor mill of accusation. Whereas the Human Rights Campaign had equipped its canvassers to deal with any number of strange and difficult circumstances—and to wrangle a monetary contribution out of it, no less—the Clinton campaign had authorized its field staff to perform a narrow range of specific activities in a highly prescribed way. "With a WHY clearly stated in an organization," Sinek says, "anyone within the organization can make a decision as clearly and accurately as the founder. A WHY provides a clear filter for decision-making." A decision can be strategic—should we embark on this project? Or tactical—how should we respond to this point of criticism? At the field level, the campaign was entirely command-and-control. Organizers were authorized to train volunteers, register voters, and mobilize registered Democrats to vote. Any public comment on the candidate or our interpretation of her perceived beliefs was out-of-bounds. This culture of confidentiality mirrored the expectations of a Fortune 500 company, which undermined the public perception of an organization seeking to inspire broad-based public support quickly and efficiently while simultaneously confronting overwhelmingly negative media coverage.

The day after Election Day 2016, our team reconvened to close down our field office, redistributing equipment and supplies to the community. Seemingly overnight, what had previously been a bustling hub of activity was once again a vacant storefront.

## Wear Your Heart on Your Sleeve

A 2016 field experiment on door-to-door canvassing, published in *Science*, demonstrates how important it is for canvassers to be prepared to have persuasive conversations with potential supporters.[20] While the study only showed definitive effects on transgender acceptance (an abortion canvass was not measurably effective), this approach to "deep canvassing" deserves further exploration.[21] Generally speaking, campaigns tend to focus on hot-button issues to motivate voters. Instead, in-depth discussions about core values can inspire voters to think about the implications of their vote in the long-term.

Using deeper conversations to motivate support is equally relevant to political campaigns as it is to mission-driven organizations. It is insufficient for an organization's defined purpose to live solely within the mind of its leaders. Guiding convictions must be explicitly spelled out for all to see. As a brand leader, you cannot allow your audience to assume why things are one way or another, or—even worse—to encourage silence as a preferred response. Your collective ideology must be clarified, simplified, and amplified, so that everyone both inside and outside your organization can hear and comprehend the power of your shared purpose at work.

Successfully leveraging ideology to advance a cause not only demands having effortless thumbs-up conversations with existing acolytes. It requires making space for criticism and doubt and equipping advocates with the foundational values that will persuade skeptics to reconsider their stance.

While many may question both his methods and his message, Donald Trump provided a clear and potent ideological call to arms. The public narrative was consumed by "her emails," and what we know now to be Russian-aided propaganda. Still, the campaign's failure to effectively communicate a positive future vision had nothing to do with Donald Trump or Russia. Hillary Clinton offered no clear ideological mandate to motivate undecided voters to support her.

By using the 2016 campaign case study in this chapter and the rest of this book, I do not intend to haggle over whether Hillary Clinton might have won in the right places if she had made different choices. America has no shortage of Monday-morning quarterbacks on that count. Hillary Clinton received three million more votes than her opponent. As previously stated, it is likely the interference of malicious foreign actors seeking to destabilize our country and in so doing disrupt the entire world order had a meaningful impact on her loss. She very well could have won.

I recognize that retrospective political accounts by campaign "insiders" can seem heedlessly salacious and self-aggrandizing. This is not my intent. My focus on the Clinton campaign is driven solely by my firsthand insight; many political campaigns repeatedly commit the same blunders. More than anything, I wish to highlight how the presence or absence of ideology can hobble or enable the efficacy of any organization. In so doing, I hope to help future brands successfully navigate similar circumstances such that they avoid making the same mistakes.

## Defining Your Ideology

Defining ideology is the first step in the Heptagon Method. The answer to the question *Why are you here?* comes from a clear understanding of shared purpose. By collaboratively defining your ideology, you can offer every single person within your organization the same level of clarity from which to act.

Building a strong foundation of vision and belief—defined by why your organization exists and the change you seek to create in the world—provides the brand compass that will guide you with clarity and confidence, regardless of how circumstance might shape your work. Ideology ultimately rests on three core truths: Where are you going? How will you get there? What guiding principles will you honor along the way? A brand's purpose is both bold and subtle. Plenty of powerful causes have created meaningful change without undertaking a lengthy workshop on organizational purpose. Alternatively, consider corporations accused of greenwashing. When an organization publicly violates the social contract, the absence of values becomes even more pronounced. While their website may proclaim a higher purpose, it only matters if the brand's behavior is compliant with its stated ideals.

To define your ideology, focus on five fundamental components, each of which is driven by a guiding question:

1. **Vision:** What is the goal you seek to achieve, and what outcome will you accomplish once you do so? What will it look like when you realize your desired outcome?
2. **Mission:** What actions and activities will you undertake to arrive at that desired result? What are you uniquely qualified to do?
3. **Values:** What guiding principles will you honor in pursuit of your goal?
4. **Personality:** How do you wish your community of brand advocates to perceive you in the process?

5. **Brand Promise:** What core delivery of value and experience will you promise to your brand advocates?

Within this book, you will sometimes find the words "brand" and "organization" used interchangeably, though they are distinct in a few important ways. The organization is the infrastructure and human resource that creates the capacity to deliver on your mission, whereas a brand is merely a consistently reinforced idea that exists in the mind of your constituent. The idea that a constituent holds is premised both on the ambitious conviction you put forward, and on your ability to achieve it. Randall Rozin calls this the brand equation, the sum of promises made over promises delivered.[22] To successfully craft a brand with impact, you must offer both an ambitious brand promise and the ability to be true to your word.

In the Heptagon Method Brand Foundations quiz, the first question we ask is: Do you know why your organization exists?[23] This might seem absurdly obvious, but if the answer to this question is in any way fuzzy, it will be helpful to begin with inquiry. Convene your stakeholders. Understand why they have supported your efforts. When have they seen it at its best? For established brands suffering from brand vagueness, documenting your organization's impact provides the raw ingredients from which to create a revitalized brand. For new or temporary initiatives (such as, say, political campaigns), the ideology can take shape in one of two ways. Leaders can document their own values and aspirations and use that frame to inspire their advocates and guide their efforts. Alternatively, an organization can seek the input of constituents to identify the values it will honor and the vision it will advance over time.

The temporary nature of modern political campaigns inherently undermines their long-term impact and the efficacy of the candidates they nominate and ultimately elect. By focusing on the tactical practices prescribed to win, campaigns often overlook the subtle foundations that can make or break their success. I expect a greater emphasis on vision and values among the Democratic Party's leadership would yield both more electoral victories and better governance. The demonstrated ability to keep their brand promise would likely inspire greater fealty among voters.

Very often, taking time to define your ideology in shared terms can seem like a distraction from taking urgent action to achieve your goals. However, clearly framing your organization's ideology provides a strong foundation from which to provide a universal understanding of your shared purpose. One thing is certain: the presence or absence of ideology will define your future impact. Without that precision, most organizations have no choice but to resort to pure profit-seeking for survival. With such clarity, brands unlock a world of possibility.

## CHAPTER 4

# Identity Brings Ideology to Life

*"In the social jungle of human existence, there is no feeling of being alive without a sense of identity."*
–Erik Erikson

In the early years of my career, I found employment in fundraising easily, thanks in part to my successful start with the Human Rights Campaign years earlier. I felt empowered by the opportunity to help mission-driven organizations raise the money they needed, but I quickly discovered the financial compensation you receive for being a successful fundraiser often comes at a cost. While raising money is necessary for mission-driven organizations to achieve their aims, fundraising tends to be a very siloed activity. Fundraising staff are often excluded from participating in the fulfillment of the mission. Your time is measured in dollars, which means you must spend it focused on raising money, but rarely on anything else. After a few years, I felt undervalued and one-dimensional. I wanted my work to be an engine for impact. While the challenges of making a career switch were considerable, I began looking for jobs that would move me into the middle of the action, directly managing programs for a forward-thinking nonprofit.

Around the time I contemplated a career change, I also began to question some of the fundamental assumptions of traditional philanthropy. Corporate Social Responsibility (known as CSR) was an increasingly visible trend among big-name brands. While some companies faced accusations of "greenwashing," using philanthropic initiatives to divert attention from the social harm caused by their production, many corporate leaders seemed genuinely interested in exploring and expanding how they might use philanthropy for real social impact. I wondered about the disruptive power of corporations leveraging their resources for good. How might strategic corporate philanthropy affect the work of nonprofit organizations? I wanted the chance to see for myself. I set my sights on an international nonprofit that helped Fortune 500 companies develop CSR programs in emerging markets. I applied for a program manager role at an organization that was then called CDC Development Solutions, later known as PYXERA Global, that would take me out of fundraising and into project planning and execution.

In his 2016 book *The Purpose Economy*, Aaron Hurst writes about the ways that the boundaries between sectors have slowly shifted over the past decade. "To move a market, we have to look beyond sector boundaries," Hurst writes.[24] While revenue is obviously critical for companies to thrive, business can no longer measure its performance simply in terms of profit. "As we move beyond sector lines," Hurst asserts, "it is increasingly difficult for business to be able to justify a myopic bottom-line strategy or for nonprofits to ignore the importance of market forces."

In just over a decade, more than 2,500 companies have voluntarily certified as B Corporations, complying with rigorous ethical and social standards to demonstrate their commitment to both profit and social impact.[25] At the same time, Fortune 500 companies have invested hundreds of millions of dollars in social impact and corporate-responsibility programs. According to Hurst, every organization must transform how it works to integrate and optimize across sector lines, guided by the directional compass that their core values and vision— their brand's meaning—provides.

My new employer was among the first to see the growing importance of cross-sector collaboration. The organization's leadership had already adjusted its vision and mission to point in this direction. But they also confronted an important transition. After more than two decades working on the front lines of international development, the brand that had captured the organization's identity for so long no longer served their mission.

While resources to support the process were limited, the leadership team agreed they needed to prioritize a complete rebranding. Ultimately, I was hired as both a program manager and the organization's sole communications employee. In this capacity, I would manage CSR programs half of the time and, in my remaining hours, coordinate the organization's rebranding effort.

Because rebranding is an opportunity to take a step back, it is wise to start this process by taking a hard look at your brand's current position and its underlying ideology. Once you have clearly defined your brand's ideological conviction (see Chapter 3), you can examine its identity. Do your brand's name and logo effectively amplify the purpose you seek to serve? If not, you will need to re-design it to do so. If your organization is new, you will move through this process for the first time. Either way, defining or redefining identity represents a critical juncture in the life of an organization. It is the moment an ideology becomes a brand. Choosing a name, logo, colors, and fonts to represent your ideology comes with a significant investment of time and talent. It often takes more time than you expect (or hope!). Yet, the investment in a new brand identity—one with integrity—almost always pays dividends.

In this chapter, we take a close look at PYXERA Global's rebranding process to understand how ideology and identity go hand-in-hand. Many people assume that "rebranding" means simply choosing a new name or designing a new logo. In truth, branding is a framing moment. It provides the opportunity to look squarely at the past and the present to clarify the future and to frame your organization's identity around the goals it seeks to pursue.

Redefining its identity from CDC Development Solutions to PYXERA Global set in motion a new trajectory toward greater impact. The successful rebranding process has yielded enormous returns to the organization. In turn, supporting the organization's rebranding taught me a great deal about building strong foundations for mission-driven brands. Deirdre White, PYXERA Global's CEO, recently shared her perspective on its implications for PYXERA Global's future impact:

"I can't overstate what I think the value was to us internally, getting on the same page in terms of who we are, and why, and what that means," White said. "I think that was so transformational for the organization, in terms of our just being able to think strategically about where we go from here."

We learn from history and experience, and as much from our mistakes as from our successes. PYXERA Global reaped extraordinary benefits and impact from a full-identity transformation. As a case study, it illustrates the interconnection between ideology and identity, and the ways that, for established brands, the past informs the future.

# From Citizens Democracy Corps to PYXERA Global

In November of 1989, following the fall of the Berlin Wall and subsequent fall of the bloc of Communist regimes that governed Eastern Europe, American leaders believed that rapid economic growth would be the best way to ensure the survival of the region's nascent democracies. The big question was: How could the United States most effectively support the region's entrance into the global free economy?

Instead of simply deploying funds, the US government decided to deploy one of America's most valuable assets, its experienced business leaders, to assist new entrepreneurs in building their nascent businesses. Known within the White House and the State Department as "the CDC" (in spite of the acronym being well-inhabited by Centers for Disease Control), Citizens Democracy Corps was founded as a nonprofit organization, independent of government. American business and organizational leaders traveled to Romania, Bulgaria, Poland, Czech Republic, Slovakia, and elsewhere to teach fledgling entrepreneurs the basics of management, marketing, and supply-chain development. By funding the deployment of skilled Volunteer Advisors (or VAs, as they came to be known), the United States effectively bypassed any bureaucracy it may have encountered in its attempts to fund the fledgling economies, instead providing technical support directly to the grassroots level of the region's economic engine: small-business entrepreneurs.

While skilled-volunteer deployment remained one of CDC's core offerings, as USAID's budget grew in the early 2000s, the organization seized opportunities to expand its work into new areas of development, pioneering programs in the field of local content and integrated community development. Soon, Citizens Democracy Corps no longer seemed an appropriate moniker.

Deirdre White joined the organization as a vice president in 2002, and immediately encouraged the leadership team to undertake a name-change process. "Even back fifteen years ago," White said, "the name was not representative of our work." The organization maintained its CDC acronym, changing its name from Citizens *Democracy* Corps to Citizens *Development* Corps, to account for the ways the organization had grown into the development space.

A few years later, something still was not quite right. The organization's portfolio had shifted again, this time away from government funding and toward the private sector. A "volunteer corps" was no longer in demand. Instead, Fortune 500 companies were looking for help developing programs to deploy their own talent into emerging markets. Moreover, the geographic reach of their work had expanded considerably. The organization needed a name that would emphasize its ability to design and deliver private-sector-led programs effectively. "CDC" had quickly become an overburdened acronym in the United States, thanks to the rising visibility of the Centers for Disease Control. But a few leaders within the organization hesitated to part with the legacy brand recognition in many countries around the world. In 2009, the organization became CDC Development Solutions, abbreviated to CDS. It does not take much scrutiny to anticipate the challenges that could arise from a brand within a brand, an acronym within an acronym, but they soldiered on.

By the time I joined the organization in 2012, the leadership of the organization had determined the extra effort required to overcome the brand's misperceptions was no longer worthwhile. It was time for a gut renovation, to leave the old CDC identity behind and forge on toward a bright, albeit uncertain, future. We began the painful, but necessary, process of building a new brand identity that better reflected the organization's work and the constituents it served.

While the organization had changed its name and updated its logo in 2009, it had not completed the vital work of understanding what the brand represented. "We hadn't gone through a strategic process," White reflected, "of what we wanted to say and to whom." More than that, CDC Development Solutions (CDS) had not reframed its ideology such that an identity with the real ring of truth remained illusory.

In hindsight, however, the problem was not so much that any of the CDC iterations were strategic failures; it was more that the organization had acquiesced to a broader challenge in the social sector. Nonprofit organizations face criticism for spending money on anything other than their "programs." A resulting culture of thrift often leads nonprofit executives to believe they are capable of doing things themselves on the cheap, rather than hiring expert consultants.

To her credit, White had spent a lot of time laying the groundwork for the change with the organization's leadership. The approval of both the executive team and the board of directors are two important steps required to make any significant change in most nonprofits. The good news is that once you have the green light from executive leadership and the board, your project is likely to go forward.

Once the leadership decided to rebrand fully, scrutiny shifted to the range of agencies able to provide support. Hiring an agency to professionally rebrand your organization almost always comes with sticker shock. The search takes patience, a great deal of determination, and a fair amount of luck. After at least a few rounds of Goldilocks—"Too big! Too small! Too expensive! Out of sync!"—we finally found an agency that our leadership team was ready to accept, the magic combination of reasonable cost and strength of capability. "I felt like they understood us," White said. "They seemed genuinely excited to help us do something interesting."

## Brand Identity Is More Than a Name

When you initiate a branding process, most people rush to a key assumption: a brand is what you call something. If you're not careful when rebranding a long-standing organization, as with the expected arrival of a newborn child, an obsession with finding the right name can eclipse everything else of importance. Each person involved rushes to offer their personal preference. Experimental naming can be cathartic for organizational leaders who are frustrated with their old brand. *If only we could think of the right word*, they think, *all of our problems would be solved.*

A brand, however, is much more than just a name. Identity comes from a brand's core values, the sentiments you seek to foster in your constituents, or the sensibility you want your services and products to evoke. When developing a new brand, it is tempting to rush to a name, instead of first taking the time to define and validate the core purpose of the brand they are seeking to build. It helps to first establish what the new brand should stand for, and then build the brand identity on the basis of ideology.

Five years later, the process of defining what the brand stood for, according to White, was still the most impactful part of the work. "I had always thought the external piece of the brand was most important," she said, "but getting a cohesive sense, internally, of who we are and what we're about was transformational."

## Finding the Identity that Does Your Ideology Justice

With help from our branding agency, the leadership team began the careful work of documenting what the brand needed to represent, the values at the core of CDS' almost twenty-five-year history. The agency undertook an extensive inquiry phase, interviewing clients, international staff, and board members to understand their experience of the brand. Through a series of interactive workshops with staff, a series of brand values and attributes emerged. Soliciting internal and external feedback validated that the results represented the real views of the organization. Using an archetypal branding process, the leadership team determined the three core archetypes we wanted the brand to reflect.

Archetypal branding is based on Carl Jung's twelve definitions of the core human personalities. Carl Jung understood archetypes as universal, archaic patterns and images that derive from the collective unconscious and which are the psychic counterpart of instinct.[26]

These include the Innocent, the Everyman, the Hero, the Nurturer, the Explorer, the Rebel, the Lover, the Creator, the Jester, the Sage, the Magician, and the Ruler. Selecting three foundational archetypes for a brand—one primary, two secondary—ensures that the brand is grounded in human aspiration and emotion, evokes a human personality, and provides an application of purpose beyond the abstract notion of its value proposition or business case.

Archetypal branding is especially helpful for crafting purposeful brands. The use of human tropes empowers people to navigate complex ideas more easily through commonly shared cultural touchstones. My specific experiences of a Lover or Jester might be distinct from yours, but our collective awareness of the distinctions between these two characters (or brands) are very similar. Rather than arguing about whether a brand value should be "courage" or "bravery," the discussion focuses on whether the brand is a Hero or a Rebel, drawing on a shared understanding of the differences between two personality types, both of which may ultimately be equally courageous. From the start, archetypal branding enables stakeholders to characterize more immediately and accurately the type of brand they want. Core beliefs flow naturally from the common understanding of the human archetypes, providing a helpful frame from which to define a mission-driven brand.

From the twelve, the CDS leadership team decided that the Magician, the Sage, and the Explorer best represented the brand:

**The Magician:** The Magician makes real what at one time might have seemed impossible. Bridging from conception to manifestation, the Magician transforms how people see the world.

**The Sage:** With the wisdom to look beyond the present to the future, the Sage uses curiosity and insight to make sense of the world. A champion for new ideas and methods that can deliver proven results, the Sage is a trusted advisor and purveyor of truth.

**The Explorer:** The Explorer forges a path of self-discovery. Often restless and ambitious, the Explorer is independent-minded and hungry for new adventures.

In most cases, there is no one right answer of which three archetypes should represent a brand. I have led workshops within organizations where different groups have chosen completely different archetypes and yet wound up with the same values. The point is to examine the human essence that underlies the brand's work. Is the brand a Nurturer? A Lover? A Ruler? The energy of each identity shapes how the brand evolves.

## From Archetypes to Core Values

Founders almost always infuse startup brands with their own core values and vision. Yet, an organization's activities can stray from their original purpose, shifting its values and attributes as a result. In the Heptagon Method, the archetypes are used to define core values that shape the voice of the brand. By defining these values first, you ensure: 1) that the name chosen appropriately conveys its core essence, and: 2) that the leaders of the organization are all operating under the same premise. It is surprising how often people within a single organization assume their values are the same, only to discover they are not.

Defining the values codifies what the organization cares about, and why. Forming values-based belief statements provides a foundation for all external communication, ensuring that a brand's purpose is present in both how and why it communicates. At the same time, it is essential to define the attributes by which the brand wants to be known. The brand personality describes how constituents and external audiences perceive the brand. A mirror of the values, the personality provides a framework to gauge how effective the brand communication is in reaching and motivating its target audience.

PYXERA Global's values focused on the global nature of the organization's scope of work, the friendliness and empathy with which it engaged with clients and partners, and the creativity and innovation it sought to foster in the domain of international development. Integrity, excellence, focus, collaboration, innovative transformation, and gentle leadership were all explicit tenets of the new brand, while its personality would be smart and inspirational, unafraid to flaunt its "rugged global flair."[27]

Many brands consider revising their mission and vision at the same time that they undertake a branding exercise. Within the Heptagon Method, these statements easily flow out of the values and personality of the organization. The mission defines how the organization does its work, the means and methods it employs to pursue its purpose. The vision defines why the organization exists, articulating the aspirational end state the brand seeks to advance.

*PYXERA Global*

*MISSION: To reinvent how public, private, and social interests engage to solve global challenges.*

*VISION: A culture of sustained collaboration that improves lives and communities worldwide.*[28]

I asked Deirdre White what surprised her most about the process. "Realizing that even within the organization, we didn't have . . . a cohesive understanding of who we are," she recalled. "The depth of the lack of cohesion was eye-opening." She specifically remembered the way the archetypes had helped her think about the brand in both a theoretical and practical way. Theoretical: What does it mean to be a Sage? Practical: How do we stack up against other well-known Explorer brands?

---

## *Then,* Finding a Name (and a Tagline)

Once you have established your brand's ideology, it is finally time to turn to the work of finding a name. Brands often confront a dilemma, choosing between the comfort of a highly explicit brand that describes exactly what the organization does, versus the mystery of an obtuse evocative brand that will allow the organization to change shape over time. Citizens Democracy Corps was the ultimate explicit brand, which had inevitably constrained the organization's ability to develop new capabilities and services.

Navigating the incremental changes within the bounds of CDC had reassured the leadership that a new, evocative name would help protect the brand from future reinvention. "An evocative brand was a good choice," White said. "The nature of the work that we are doing to solve big global problems doesn't lend itself well to easy description. Having a name that could evolve with us and didn't constrain us was really important."

Naming is a tricky business for a number of reasons, and CDS Development Solutions faced a particularly difficult circumstance. The new name needed to work in Spanish, Portuguese, French, Arabic, Russian, Turkish, and a handful of African and Asian languages, too. The agency brought reams and reams of names each week, but inevitably for each one, a flaw emerged. One name sounded like a word that meant "outsider" in Portuguese. Another meant "penis" in French. Another meant "beggar" in Sanskrit. Any words containing the letters J, K, or Z would be highly problematic in Arabic.

In seeking a new name, any organization faces a growing list of constraints. Nothing too cute! But not too serious, either! Make sure it can be readily understood, but also, it should sound smart. While the consideration factors continued to mount, the options remain scarce. The truth is, there really is nothing new under the sun. If you think you have a delightfully perfect name for your organization and its work, odds are someone, somewhere, is doing something under a similar banner. Check for intellectual-property competition. Focus on utility. Does the name sound nice? Is it appropriate for your audience? Does it accurately convey your purpose or some key component of your vision? Is it sufficiently flexible to absorb changes in your mission over time? If the answer to most of these questions is "yes," you probably have a winner. Remember it is more a flower vase than a sculpture, designed to hold the beautiful bouquet of projects and initiatives you will create to achieve your mission, not to stand on its own. Its utility as a container is more important than its individual perfection.

For legacy brands whose ideology has outgrown an outdated name, the decision to invest in identity can be even more difficult. It can be hard to justify sinking an old ship and building a new one. So much love and care have gone into its maintenance over the years. Yet so many organizations have unlocked new success and visibility by investing in new identities. Aesthetic styles change over time, as do naming trends. All successful brands—even Coca-Cola, IBM, Google, and Microsoft—make investments in updating their identities to suit the times. Successful mission-driven organizations should not hesitate to do the same.

After several weeks of failing to come up with a brand that "felt right," we finally landed on an idea that resonated. We got very close to launching the brand, only to discover an IP conflict. "I wish I had known to get the lawyers involved earlier in vetting names," White lamented. We went back to the drawing board to find a new, equally serviceable name. Ultimately, we chose a fusion of two words: *pyxis*, the Greek word for a navigational device, and *terra*, Latin for earth, which together form pyx-era. PYXERA Global was born.

Once a name is determined, it is time to turn to the tagline. Often used to underwrite the name and logo, the tagline is the third most-visible element of a brand. It provides a simple framing of the organization's mission and vision in three to eight words. Because we had selected an evocative name, we opted for an explicit tagline: *The New Frontier of Global Engagement.*

## The Next Circle of Hell (Designing a Logo)

Every branding agency will tell you a logo-design process should take one concept round with three rounds of revision to follow. It always takes more. Naming is extraordinarily difficult, but logo development is a close second. While establishing a strong and clear ideology helps ensure the general direction of the brand, designing a new logo inevitably devolves into a lopsided process of one step forward, two steps back, until you are hobbling in a circle.

Kidding. (Sort of.)

Having decided the name and the tagline, we were ready for the logo-design stage. The process took five rounds. "I remember just not liking a lot of things," White recalled, laughing. The first-round logo resembled a multicolor speedometer. The second, a series of directional arrows. I do not remember the substance of the subsequent rounds, but by the fourth round, we began to feel empathy for Hansel and Gretel, wandering around in the woods. Like most things, arriving at an inspiring logo requires creativity, persistence, and a little bit of luck.

The team was almost ready to settle for mediocrity when the final logo arrived. "In the last round," she said, "they came back with a logo that so perfectly represents the complexity of what we do."

Ultimately, the logo became a beautiful, multidimensional, globe compass. The day we launched the brand, and I was finally allowed to hand out my new business cards, I hosted an after-hours event in my office for an outside group. Our speaker that night arrived a few minutes early, and I took the opportunity to hand him a card. He looked at it thoughtfully for a moment, before smiling and saying, brightly, "Oh, I see. It's like the earth—in colors!"

"Yes!" I said. "Exactly!" Victory.

## Planning Your Brand Entrance

Of course, before you get to the brand launch, there is plenty of ground yet to cover. After a great deal of fatigue from the naming and logo-development processes, our team barely had the patience for the final details, but these elements of the brand were no less important. Everything from colors and fonts to website copy had to be completely reimagined to reflect the ideology and identity of the new brand.

We wanted a logo font that would convey the classical origin of the name, alluding to the navigational nature of our work, and colors that were rich and bright. We selected blue, green, and orange to convey the public, private, and social sectors collaborating around the world. We labored over every detail: the exact shades of color within the logo; the precise tones used for the text of the name; how the words of the name would correspond to one other, relative to the logo's position.

We spent weeks developing the new website, drafting email announcements, and reviewing collateral assets to educate staff and clients about the new organizational identity. It was imperative to ensure everyone had the tools to understand the process of transformation we had just undertaken and to prepare them to speak with one voice on behalf of and about the new brand. With help from the agency, we created Word and PowerPoint templates, as well as a one-page brand-summary sheet. At monthly staff meetings, White would call on members of the team to recall the mission, vision, and brand attributes, inviting people to share examples of the brand's attributes in action. Slowly, the brand transformed from a theoretical framework into a lived experience.

## Leading the Brand . . . the Rest of the Way

Once the logo and brand guide were complete, it was time to integrate these new values and themes into outward-facing brand collateral. We undertook a comprehensive website overhaul and new collateral development. Over the next several years, the leadership made strategic investments in events and sponsorships to strategically position the new brand. Two years later, PYXERA Global's twenty-fifth anniversary became a pinnacle point of global engagement and visibility.

Looking back, five key factors contributed to the success of PYXERA Global's rebranding process:

1. **Executive Leadership:** The active involvement of the CEO from the start was critical to the project's success. Getting the endorsement of PYXERA Global's board before the process began ensured the acceptance of the final outcome. Deirdre White ensured that the board and leadership team stayed abreast of progress and that resources were prioritized to support the process from beginning to end.

2. **Hiring the Right Agency:** Hiring a right-fit agency was critical to ensuring the project's success. In this case, the agency's innovative, mission-driven approach ensured the organization focused

appropriately on integrating core beliefs into the brand's development. While one may scrutinize the cost of hiring outside support, the value of getting it right is ultimately worth it.

3. **An Internal Champion:** It is vital to have not just the right agency, but also a staff person who is committed to the success of the project and who has the time and focus to keep it moving forward. In this case, that person was me, a dedicated brand champion. I was responsible for coordinating the involvement of both the agency and the leadership team to ensure appropriate engagement at each stage of the process.

4. **Living the Brand:** Staff engagement in any branding project is especially important for mission-driven brands. Focusing staff time on brand development, however, will likely mean sidelining other operational priorities for a time. Yet, this is essential for a couple of reasons. First, the collaborative participation of staff increases their shared sense of ownership and ensures the end product truly represents the organization's values. Second, staff involvement is necessary for those within the organization to gain the confidence required to project the new identity out into the world.

5. **Amplifying the Brand:** Once the ideology and identity were complete, it took many more hours of staff time to develop new language to describe services and initiatives and to launch a new website. It took additional time and effort to project it outward and ensure its broader visibility and relevance. Creating the brand was only the first step in a long process of outward expression, which is addressed more fully in Chapters 6 and 7.

Once you have decided to invest in a new identity, use your ideology to define your brand. Without that focus, the quest for the right name and logo will rest primarily on the subjective preferences of your team, which can be frustrating. ("I like blue . . ." "Well, I prefer teal . . ." Stalemate.) Instead, focus on the feelings you hope a name and logo will evoke in your audience, how effectively they convey your values and vision, and what a first-time viewer would think or feel upon first exposure.

As you embark on this step of the journey, also consider that additional benefits lie hidden within the process itself. Rebranding represents an opportunity to bring stakeholders together, to consult them on their past experience of the brand and their hopes for future impact. Even if the ideology has already been set by the organization's leadership team, asking staff, board members, and other constituents for input into the process can inspire even greater loyalty and support for the new brand.

As White reflected on the enormous amount of time and energy PYXERA Global spent on its rebranding, she also considered how the process had shaped the future prospects of the organization. As a direct result of better understanding its brand identity, PYXERA Global developed an ambitious but deeply aligned five-year strategy that honored the rich history and core values of the organization. "Getting on the same page through this rebranding process has allowed us to think differently and strategically for the organization," White affirmed. By daring to depart from the past, White and her leadership team opened up a whole new world of possibility, planting seeds of industry-wide influence that would soon come to bear fruit.

## CHAPTER 5

# Getting from Meaning to Message

*"Whether you think you can or whether you think
you cannot, you are right."*
–Henry Ford

Before beginning my work at PYXERA Global, I had reached a point of professional frustration. It was the summer of 2012, and I was desperate. I had changed jobs only six months before, and found myself unexpectedly stuck and looking for a way out. I started looking for pathways that might lead to something new. "Startups" were in the zeitgeist, but no one quite knew what made a startup successful, or how or why they succeeded or failed. These new engines of industry seemed to provide a mythical pathway out of the everyday boredom of the mundane nine-to-five lifestyle.

While I had yet to land on a big, bold idea that would justify a startup of its own, I thought optimistically about joining someone else's new venture as a co-founder, but I had no idea how to find one. Working in the social sector in Washington, DC, I hadn't the faintest idea how to discover such an opportunity. A brief Google search led me to the Lean Startup Machine, a weekend-long workshop in downtown DC that promised the opportunity to "build a successful business in three days."[29] For $199, I signed up immediately.

Around that same time, I also became aware of human-centered design, an emerging practice increasingly applied to the development of innovative solutions to social problems. Straight from Wikipedia:

> *Human-centered design (HCD) is a design and management framework that develops solutions to problems by involving the human perspective in all steps of the problem-solving process. Human involvement typically takes place in observing the problem within context, brainstorming, conceptualizing, developing, and implementing the solution.*[30]

In addition, HCD relies on a process of rapid iteration, leveraging a minimum viable product to gain user feedback that can immediately help make the solution more effective. IDEO, one of the first companies to champion the approach, had just released its first HCD Field Guide, a 180-page document that led people through the steps in the method.

However, human-centered design was hard to learn by simply reading about in a book. I was seeking opportunities to gain more hands-on understanding, and Lean Startup Machine seemed like a good beginning. Though I had yet to realize it, what I would actually learn over the course of the weekend was the deep importance of customer profiling and engagement.

I arrived at the designated location on a Friday evening, at 6 p.m. Participants trickled in, making handwritten name tags, and nibbling slices of greasy pizza. At 6:30, the official program commenced. Each person had thirty seconds to pitch an idea. If you did not yet have an idea—no pressure!—you could listen to everyone else. Following the pitch session, the group of fifty or more participants had fifteen minutes to organize into teams to work on our favorite ideas. MOOCs—massive open online courses—were in their infancy; Coursera had been founded only months before. I wound up aligned to an idea for a platform called Quume, designed to provide a badging system that would allow people to get public credit for learning completed online.

Our challenge: in forty-eight hours, build enough structure behind your business to gain currency. Currency, in startup land, means the willingness of a user to pay you money for the use of your good or service. Beyond the startup teams that were each working on a different idea, the room was filled with mentors, experienced technologists, and developers who had firsthand experience developing new businesses. They provided both general recommendations and personalized advice: Use Survey-Monkey to get user feedback. Use Unbounce to create a landing page. Use Google AdWords to see which landing-page performs better. More than anything else, get out of the building and talk to your prospective customer.

The premise of Lean Startup Machine was to document and (in)validate your assumptions, to work from real customer feedback rather than the experience of the entrepreneurs. Teams developed questionnaires and set out on Saturday morning for Dupont Circle or the National Mall—anywhere they could find humans they could ask about their product or service. While the business-model canvass has now become an established part of startup culture, in 2012 it was still relatively new.[31] The canvass was designed to help you outline your customer, your cost structure, and your potential revenue. In other words, who is paying for what? But before anyone paid for anything, you had to have something to sell.

Here, the relationship between the service and the customer was the key. As smartphones were becoming mainstream, apps were emerging as a solution to just about anything. Startup founders were quick to decide that their own interest in an app meant that a customer would want it, too. This, I would come to learn, was a premature assumption. Customers will often Ooooh and Aaaahhh about a new thing. They will nod their heads and say, "Oh yes, I like that!" But that does not mean they are ready to pay for anything. The goal was not simply to get a nod of approval. It was understanding whether you were actually solving the customer's problem. What service is the customer hiring you to provide? And are they willing to spend actual cash for it?

## GOOB: The Silly Four-Letter Acronym That Changed How I Think About Messaging

In the Lean Startup workshop, a funny four-letter acronym became the driving motivation: GOOB—Get Out of the Building. Only by getting outside and talking to real people can you understand the real challenges they face, and whether the solution you have in mind will address them.

I learned that understanding the person you are trying to serve is a key step in advancing your audience's engagement with a new idea. To capture the essence of the person you are trying to serve, it is helpful to create a persona (sometimes called an avatar or profile) that offers generic specificity about a customer's preferences and behavior. Generic specificity—a nice oxymoron. The point is that the persona should be based on a real person and convey specific characteristics ("enjoys smartphone games like Words with Friends" or "drinks coffee from Peet's, not Starbucks") that can help you envision a person with a specific point of view.

A good persona begins with an empathy map.[32] Ideally, a persona is built based on an interaction with a real person (like those GOOB conversations). The conversation is not meant to determine if the customer likes a specific solution. Instead, it is meant to help you unpack a customer's desires. What does this person love? What does she want more than anything in the world? What does she absolutely hate? What is she most afraid of? A clear understanding of these key elements of a customer's point of view makes designing a solution that meets their needs and effectively marketing that solution to them much more straightforward.

For mission-driven organizations, the word "customer" may be confusing or even slightly off-putting. But the term "customer" in this case connotes the person who provides currency. Whether you are soliciting donations or selling a product or service, the big question is the same:

*Why should this person want to give you money, time, or attention for what you are doing?*

Quite often, mission-driven organizations become so mission-focused that they lose sight of the revenue model required to make the work possible. You may assume that by simply doing the work, people will flock to your cause. But that is rarely the case. We all want to live in a world made just for us. It is your job as a brand leader to create that world for your customers.

While desirable, it is not enough to build a brand wrought with purpose. The best mission-driven brands, those that become catalysts for change, empower everyone in the organization to communicate with the same conviction and resolve as their leadership. This often means turning ideology into everyday statements—brand messaging—that every person within the organization can use to express, effectively and succinctly, the shared conviction of the organization. Streamlining how you express your brand's essence allows those within the organization to more effectively amplify it outward.

## Benefits of Finding the Right Message

Honing the brand message has two primary benefits. First, unifying how people communicate on behalf of your brand ensures that employees and ambassadors alike are representing it accurately and articulately. Second, and perhaps more importantly, sharpening the message helps those speaking on behalf of the brand to feel proud and confident about the organization they represent. Unlike brands that rely on manipulation tactics to compete on features and price, purpose-driven brands offer evidence and examples for why their organization exists. Doing so brings people who share the same values and convictions into the brand's community of support.

Once you know who your customer is, once you have mined and defined their deepest desires, and you understand how to solve their problem, it is time to build the value proposition. At this stage, the source material you developed while defining your ideology becomes the messaging you tailor to your audience. This can feel uncomfortable. Is it fake, someone might say, to tell your customer exactly what they want to hear?

The short answer is no, definitely not. The long answer is more nuanced. It is helpful to think of your brand as a person. Consider yourself. You might wear different clothes on a date than you do to Sunday supper with your grandmother, right? You have a different set of outfits for work as opposed to yoga class. It is possible to express yourself differently in specific settings in a way that remains authentic to you. Targeting your messaging to your audience is like choosing appropriate clothing based on the occasion. Instead of thinking of this as inauthentic, it is more helpful to think of it as brand emphasis. There will be specific elements of your brand values that will resonate with certain segments of your audience more than others. You can emphasize the components that are most inspiring to them without deviating from your brand's core truth.

As we have seen, a great deal happens in step 1: ideology, and step 2: identity, defining mission, vision, and values, choosing a name, and creating a logo. These action-packed steps are exciting and inspiring for internal stakeholders. The message step, however, is more of a strategic-positioning exercise focused on understanding your target audience and finding the key themes that inspire their allegiance to the brand. Rather than serving as a manipulation tactic, targeted messaging allows you to showcase the specific element of your brand that most resonates with a specific stakeholder.

At the message step in the Heptagon Method, our focus shifts away from defining the core of the brand itself—the vision, mission, and values that express what the brand does and why it exists—to determining how the brand attributes inspire different audience segments. At this point, the brand values, in particular, serve as a helpful aid. By identifying all of the things that your brand stands for, and explaining them in a sentence or two, you can codify your deeply held convictions in a way that is conducive to your customer's preferences. If your brand values are, say, courage, transparency, and integrity, you can emphasize each of these aspects of your brand values to different audience segments. One set of donors may care a great deal about courage, while another may be much more interested in how you are safeguarding integrity. Perhaps neither "courage" nor "integrity" will appear in your brand's mission or vision statements—the most visible parts of the ideology. A strategically oriented brand, however, can subtly bring these brand attributes to life in its communication without explicitly using those terms. In so doing, you can form a deeper connection with your stakeholders that is based on shared values, which motivates a commitment to your brand.

## Creating a Brand Message That Resonates

Start by interviewing a diverse range of stakeholders (six to ten). Ask them questions about their life experiences. Ask them to articulate what challenges they are most motivated to solve. Ask them what values shape their commitment to charitable giving or volunteer engagement. Empathize with your customers to understand them. Then, take these insights and consider them in the context of your organization's defined values. Can you draw connections between explicit values and specific customers?

Evaluating a person's empathy map can help you determine which emotion is most likely to motivate them to act on your behalf. For example, you may decide that your brand's commitment to courage helps your donors feel confident. Alternatively, perhaps your commitment to transformation makes them feel inspired. Clearly understanding each audience segment's beliefs allows you to hone your message and choose stories that resonate with their core values. Once you have analyzed how your ideology lines up with customer preferences, use it as a framework to guide your communication.

You can sum up the process of crafting a multi-stake-holder message in three steps:

- **Empathize:** Identify the desires that define your customer
- **Strategize:** Understand how your ideology makes them feel
- **Amplify:** Position your meaning to inspire your customer to care

The rest of this chapter explores how these three steps can help you communicate with your audience more effectively. Keep in mind that messaging is often more strategic than action-centered. You will rarely amplify key messages to your audience directly. Instead, it becomes the frame by which you will identify and prioritize the stories you share. Your message is also a hypothesis to be validated by your diverse advocates, more than it is an irrefutable truth. Chapter 9 will bring all of these concepts together with specific steps you can take to empower your advocates to take action effectively.

## Messaging Made Simple

Shortly after the Lean Startup workshop, I began my work at CDC Development Solutions. At the same time I was coordinating PYXERA Global's brand transformation, explored in depth in Chapter 4, I was simultaneously responsible for PYXERA Global's communication. Before the launch of the new brand, however, the organization lacked an effective communications platform. Its website was more than four years old and was badly outdated. The new brand would take more than a year to launch. While the work to build the new brand and its requisite collateral was underway, there was no clear way to tell the stories of the organization's ongoing impact.

When setting out to create a solution to your customer's problem, it is natural to want to offer them perfection. Lean Startup, however, taught me the opposite. In truth, what you are after is an MVP—a Minimum Viable Product. Instead of offering the customer all the bells and whistles right up front, the MVP offers the customer the simplest possible version of the remedy to their problem. Starting simple strips away the bright-shiny-object syndrome that can arise from solutions that look nice but fail to deliver.

The MVP gives way to the rapid prototype, the simplest version of the solution you can make as quickly as humanly possible. You might not be able to build a website in twenty minutes, but you can probably diagram your desired interface on a few pieces of paper. Show that illustration to a customer and see what they say.

Still high on the idea of the MVP in my first few months at PYXERA Global, I considered my options. What if we built a simple storytelling platform? A simple site without all of the in-depth material one would find on an organization's website, but that effectively highlighted the way the brand was already delivering on its mission. To fill the gap, I proposed launching an online magazine. Developed on a shoestring, *The New Global Citizen* had three mandates. First, the publication offered a stop-gap outreach channel that would also create a red-carpet effect for the new organizational identity still in development. Second, it focused on the key themes on which PYXERA Global wanted to amplify expertise and experience. Most importantly, perhaps, it provided a broad umbrella under which PYXERA Global could become a convener within the domain of corporate social responsibility and global development.

While its overall focus was human stories of impact, the magazine was designed to address five key themes: Global Pro Bono, Citizen Diplomacy, Enterprise Development, Impact & Innovation, and Leadership. Each of these themes was a calling card for a specific segment of PYXERA Global's audience. Global Pro Bono represented PYXERA Global's largest practice. Here, we encouraged program participants to write about their experiences on the ground in countries around the world, to share both the extraordinary impact their teams had on the organizations they worked with and the effect their month-long residencies in Brazil, South Africa, India, and elsewhere had on their own personal and professional development. Citizen Diplomacy specifically engaged members of PYXERA Global's Center for Citizen Diplomacy, a previously independent nonprofit, acquired by CDC Development Solutions in 2012. This theme spoke to the benefits of people-to-people engagement and the unique benefits of cross-cultural exchange. Enterprise Development shared the stories of programs in Ghana and Mozambique focused on helping would-be entrepreneurs to start businesses, ensuring their support from large oil and gas extraction projects. These three categories captured PYXERA Global's entire portfolio of work at the time.

In addition, two categories provided a broad umbrella for big ideas that emerged in the domain of international development. Impact & Innovation (two terms not particularly favored by PYXERA Global's leadership but preferred by our target readers) made space to communicate about new ideas in the field. Leadership specifically targeted the leaders of government, development agencies, and the CEOs of Fortune 500 companies. Deirdre White and other organizational leaders penned pieces that encouraged vision and championed fortitude on the new frontier of global engagement.

Of course, not every organization needs a five-themed publication to reach its target audience. In fact, it can be beneficial to simplify the number of audiences you are trying to reach. If the community of people is too big and diverse, it can be difficult to tell the stories needed to amplify a targeted message for that audience. It is natural to want to attempt to be all things to all people, but that is often a losing strategy. Being the right thing to the right person is both more straightforward and more effective.

When thinking about the connection between people and messaging, it is important to push yourself to empathize with their likes, dislikes, wants, and fears. Too often, skin-deep characteristics like race and gender serve as proxies for customer preferences that offer weak foundations for communication.

Codifying their experience into a clear, shared understanding of who your stakeholders are and why they believe in your work is helpful and clarifying for every single person within your organization. Cultivating deep empathy with your audience reminds you and your team that the people you serve have feelings, just like the rest of us. A persona-development exercise can help orient everyone toward improving your stakeholder's experience of your brand.

Current events or changing industry trends may significantly influence your brand's message. While your audience personas and brand messages should be somewhat evergreen, it can be helpful to revisit them on a semiregular basis. Hold an internal meeting each year to resurface the personas. Ask your team if your audience's needs and desires still seem accurate. Even better: assign team members to verify these assumptions by way of a check-in call.

If you revise your personas, be sure to also revisit your messages. By equipping your team with targeted messaging that speaks to the interests and needs of specific audience segments, each person in your organization becomes empowered to speak with the unified voice of the brand. If they face objections or concerns, each person clearly understands the components of the ideology they should emphasize in their response.

## Messaging Always Goes Back to Ideology

Fast forward four years to the fall of 2016 and the Clinton campaign. The absence of foundational ideology behind the campaign hindered a targeted, substantive message. In addition to registering voters and turning them out to vote, our team distributed "chum" (yes, the metaphorical equivalent of what you feed sharks). In exchange for your time, volunteers received free campaign collateral they could proudly display on the bumpers of their cars, on their front lawns, and in shop windows. This promotional material included a collection of placards. While some were inspiring riffs on the candidate's favorite Methodist teaching—"Do the most good"—or on the "woman-card" theme—"Deal Me In!"—the rest were simply identity monikers: Seniors for Hillary, Jews for Hillary, Hispanics for Hillary, African Americans for Hillary, Haitians for Hillary.[33] The explicit assumption was that these people cared about electing Hillary Clinton because of their identity alone.

Politics offers an interesting framework from which to evaluate the power of marketing to motivate people to act. Political parties, while increasingly unpredictable and diffuse, have for decades motivated their members to vote for a chosen candidate. As party identity has fractured, however, the personality and qualifications of candidates have grown in importance while a clear ideology—especially values—have faded from view. Candidates run on their experience and expertise, as well as on the policies they promise to champion once elected. "Because I have done X, you should trust me to do Y." The candidate's charisma is often a chief quality evaluated by commentators and the voting public alike. For Hillary Clinton, however, neither her experience, expertise, nor charisma were sufficient to inspire enough voters in the right states. Her wonky policy promises were drowned out by the salacious coverage of "her emails."

Her opponent, by contrast, snubbed established methods of electioneering. He was unconcerned that his professional profile did not fit the mold of past candidates. He ignored the rigor required to formulate complex policy solutions. With a clear understanding of the audience he was seeking to reach, he laid out simple promises that realized his audience's desires and allayed their fears. Ignore for a moment that most of his proposals were unrealistic or un-American. The solutions he championed spoke directly to the prevailing lived experience and values of white working-class Americans.

Following the election of Donald Trump people often asked, incredulously, how it was that America could elect such a man as its president. The months I spent in the politically purple territory of Florida helped clarify the answer to this question. Voters, certainly in America though likely in the rest of the world, do not vote on the basis of fact. They do not vote for hypothetical future policy promises. Voters cast their ballots on one criterion alone: how the candidate makes them feel. Cost of living in America has continued to rise while real wages have stagnated. As a result, many Americans are fearful about their own economic stability and angry about rising inequality, both of which made them especially vulnerable to Donald Trump's empty promises and scare tactics.[34] Narratives perpetuated by Fox News, Breitbart, and Alex Jones only added fuel to the flame of American discontent.

A plurality of Americans had been boiling in anger over the ineptitude of government for the better part of the last decade. Trump's policy solutions stood as proxies for beliefs both he and his supporters shared: that Mexican Americans are responsible for the loss of US jobs, that Muslims are terrorists, that the US government deserves to be strategically dismantled from the inside out. Few people viewed these proposals as real solutions to the problem. Instead, they were signals of the shared values of the candidate and his base. Donald Trump recognized their fear and despair, and made them feel validated. Hillary Clinton, for all her expertise and experience, for all her well-conceived policies and plans, was unable to inspire feeling and emotional connection with enough voters in the states where it mattered most.

A few important caveats: remember that Hillary Clinton outperformed Donald Trump by more than three million votes, in spite of the ways leading voices in the media objectively undermined her standing with a seemingly unending focus on "her emails." Russian agents and Cambridge Analytica, aided by Facebook and $1.4 billion in dark money, helped the propaganda of the right drown out efforts by the Clinton campaign to amplify its own message. You may believe that the election of Donald Trump was illegal and unjust. You may wake up every day in despair about the future of America under the leadership of such a man. All of these feelings are completely valid. Yet, this reaction need not prevent us from realizing the marketing prowess his campaign exhibited, and learning from it. (Barack Obama used similar marketing on the political left. "Yes We Can!" and "Change We Can Believe In" were simply a more progressive, positive corollary to the demand to "Make America Great Again.")

It is also important to remember that your work can rarely advance in a vacuum. Thinking back to the Lean Startup Machine workshop, I realize that our project was not remarkably successful. In many ways, we failed to "Get Out of the Building." Yet the pressure to create something out of nothing within such a short timeline clarified how much time many organizations waste discussing an idea's prospects first, rather than simply putting a prototype out there to see how people respond. The best way to test your audience's interests is to create an offer and see who buys it.

The Lean Startup Machine workshop introduced me to Eric Ries's seminal book, *The Lean Startup: How Today's Entrepreneurs Use Continuous Innovation to Create Radically Successful Businesses.*[35] The book's methods, which have yielded enormous disruption and positive change within thousands of companies, has given way to Ries's new book, *The Startup Way.*[36] The Lean Startup points to three engines of growth: paid, viral, and sticky. Paid growth means that new customers cost advertising dollars. Viral growth means every one of your customers brings you five, ten, or a hundred more. Sticky growth, however, is the foundation of sustainable progress. Instead of constantly seeking new customers, sticky growth depends on loyal users and advocates. Brands that can build a sticky-growth model build a bloc of allies who care about your mission and keep coming back again and again.

"When a company clearly communicates their WHY, what they believe, and why they believe what they believe," Simon Sinek points out, "then we will sometimes go to extraordinary lengths to include those products or brands in our lives." By defining and widely communicating your ideology through your message, you both motivate and empower your audience to amplify your cause and support your goals. An ideology and empathy-driven message helps make your brand stickier, and therefore more effective.

Take Patagonia, for example, a company widely known as a pioneer in corporate social responsibility and environmental sustainability. Seeking to lead the outdoor and adventure apparel industry in durable products made from sustainably sourced fibers, the company has prioritized sharing its purpose with its customers through multiple content channels.[37] Some Patagonia customers may be more concerned with the wages and working conditions of factory workers, while others may be more interested in understanding how and where Patagonia sources the materials it uses to make its products. Some customers may be less concerned with corporate responsibility and more interested in nature; the company's recent documentary, *Fishpeople*, seeks to highlight how the ocean creates both livelihoods and adventure for people around the world. Patagonia also encourages customers to "Speak Up for Public Lands," to protect national parks and monuments from being opened to commercial development.[38] Each of these content channels amplifies a different message to a different customer segment, but each clearly supports Patagonia's mission:

"Build the best product, cause no unnecessary harm, use business to inspire and implement solutions to the environmental crisis."[39]

Brands are driven by human effort on two sides: those who advance the mission, and those who benefit directly from it. The sooner your team can interact with brand advocates to understand their deepest needs, the more easily the brand can effectively meet them. Taking time to appreciate the human experience that powers your brand's impact is often the most overlooked and potent step you can take in ensuring success for your marketing efforts.

Together, *ideology, identity,* and *message* comprise your brand's foundation. You will want to ensure each of these components of your brand is strong before setting out to amplify your brand and engage for change. Having these three elements in place provides the bedrock for successful storytelling, amplification, and, ultimately, engagement. It may be possible for a brand to succeed without all three being clearly defined, but a lack of clarity on any of them can create obstacles and inefficiency in how you communicate. By taking the time required to build effective foundations, a brand can much more easily achieve its mission and drive its community to act on its behalf. Want to figure out where your brand might need work? Head on over to the Heptagon Brand Assessment to get started: https://goo.gl/vDAXxY.

## CHAPTER 6

# The Terrible Truth About Stories That Stick

*"We tell ourselves stories in order to live."*
–Joan Didion

Perched on a cinder block, surrounded by flood water on all sides, I marveled at my circumstance. It was August 2013 and just twenty-four hours before, I had been asleep in my own bed in Washington, DC. I now found myself following a line of strangers across a flash flood in the northern suburbs of Dakar, Senegal. The few street lights were dark—seemingly, the flood had taken out the power supply. Only by the dim light of a cell phone behind me could I barely make out the next cinder block ahead. I thought momentarily of the nightmare scenario that could befall an American woman hopping across flood waters on her first night in West Africa, but I was keenly aware these strangers I had met only hours before were truly kindred spirits.

The PYXERA Global brand was weeks away from launch. While coordinating the development of the new brand, I was also managing global pro bono programs, which was how I found myself traversing flood waters in Senegal. With what remained of my time, I was also the editor of PYXERA Global's online magazine, *The New Global Citizen*.

The magazine was designed to aggregate and amplify the human experience of social impact, as well as convey key insights from the sector. We hoped that by showcasing the values and actions of specific leaders and the outcomes of a diverse range of productions, we could inspire others to engage in similar work. According to Marshall Ganz, a senior lecturer at the Kennedy School of Government at Harvard University, grounding a story in the right values can produce emotion in the listener or reader that compels them to act. Ganz has conducted a great deal of seminal work on how stories shape leaders and their ability to motivate their constituents. He calls the discipline Public Narrative: "The art of translating values into action through stories."[40] Whereas inertia, apathy, fear, isolation, and self-doubt can inhibit a person's motivation to take action, urgency, anger, hope, solidarity, and a you-can-make-a-difference attitude serve as action motivators. *The New Global Citizen* was designed to encourage those seeking to have a positive global impact.

## A Challenge. A Choice. An Outcome.

Every great story needs three things: a hero, a hurdle, and a happy ending. Ganz is more objective. He asserts that a challenge, a choice, and an outcome provide the framework for inspiring stories. The most effective brand leaders hone their ability to tell three specific stories: The Story of Self, the Story of Us, and the Story of Now.

Compelling stories transform how organizations communicate. Stories are powerful tools that can explain an organization's impact. Instead of facts and figures, stories depend on human truth to create empathy and engagement. Stories also animate the people and personalities doing great work, and appeal to emotions that will motivate others. Human brains are wired to use stories as the foundation of memory formation. Whereas facts can confuse or lose a listener, stories provide a through-line for otherwise unassociated facts, and a sense of inevitability. [41] Mission-driven work demands a systems-level awareness of the impact of a potential solution. Stories have the power to convey the systemic nature and value of a solution in ways that facts, figures, and diagrams cannot.

As the editor of *The New Global Citizen*, I spent many hours coaching people through storytelling. I wrote down guidelines designed to help people tell their stories more easily. I spent phone calls listening to people tell their stories aloud to help them write them down more effectively. I wrote outlines shaped by questions designed to make personal storytelling flow. Almost organically, the platform became a channel for amplifying the stories of Self, Us, and Now in the context of corporate social responsibility (CSR) and social impact.

Humans are inherently narrative creatures. For thousands of years we have relied on stories, like those expressed in the Bible and other ancient texts, to convey our shared values and common experiences. "Because we are gifted with episodic memory," Ganz says, "we can imagine ourselves in the scene described."[42] Ganz argues that the specific details of a story help to move the listener, articulating shared values, what philosopher Charles Taylor calls our "moral sources."[43]

Recent sociological research has shown the effect that stories have on the human brain. Hearing a story causes mirror neurons to fire in the brain such that it is as though the listener has experienced the event personally. For example, a harrowing story of survival, told in vivid detail, might bring tears to the listener's eyes as the moment comes to life in their imagination. The mirror-neuron response provides a strong foundation for human empathy, allowing each of us to understand others more fully and deeply.

Over the past five years, multimedia has evolved at an astonishing rate. While in 2013 it was cutting edge to launch a long-form storytelling platform, to-day consumers increasingly prefer audio, video, and other multimedia communication. Now you must make strategic choices—and resource allocations—to support the development of podcasts, web series, and YouTube videos. Choosing the right medium for the right story—designed to reach the correct target audience segment—is its own strategic art form.

As a result, story strategy becomes a critical step in the Heptagon Method, bridging from the strategic foundations of meaning, identity, and message to express the brand promise to the wider world. Messages do not easily stand on their own. Stories, Ganz says, "are not messages, sound bites, or brands, although these rhetorical fragments may reference a story."[44] Nesting a brand's message within a story makes it more accessible to constituents. Brand strategy also involves making strategic choices about which storytellers to empower (CEOs versus volunteers) and which media can best reach a specific audience. For example, an op-ed in a highly regarded or widely read newspaper might garner attention from a well-read older audience, whereas a video will better capture the imagination of a younger audience. Beyond these tactical realities, stories can inspire advocates to envision the action they can take on behalf of a brand, making the case for why future action is both necessary and powerful, and emphasizing the power of the community preparing to act.

## The Story of Self

The first time I heard someone tell his Story of Self in an unabashed and honest way, it caught me completely by surprise. A strange narrative loophole had suddenly come full circle. In January 2013, I attended a board leadership workshop at which Laveen Naidu, Executive Director of Dance Theatre of Harlem (DTH), spoke of his experience rescuing the company from near bankruptcy ten years before. I had seen DTH's last performance as a college student and was eager to share my joy at the company's return. Two years passed before we found time to connect.

I told him about *The New Global Citizen*, and asked if he might like to write a story. He was bashful, adamant that he had always been more of a physical communicator than one for pen and paper, but I persuaded him he was up to the task. On the phone the following week, the conversation meandered through a series of arcane topics, Naidu clearly lost in thought and trying to speak his way through to a kernel of truth. I was having trouble keeping the thread. And then—

"When DTH broke the Apartheid integration ban at Civic Theatre in Johannesburg, Nelson Mandela was in the audience—"

I could hardly believe what I was hearing. "I'm sorry," I said. "Can you say that again?"

And there it was. The moment, in 1992, when DTH's role in the world had fundamentally shifted from just another American ballet company to a change-making force. Naidu and twenty-four other performers had been the first to break the cultural barrier of Apartheid on the Civic Theatre stage. *Nelson Mandela* was in the audience.

"Do you have pictures of that?" I asked.

"I'm sure the DTH archives do," he said.

*Jackpot.*

That moment of performance was significant for him—*I can still remember the opening trills of the flutist*, he later wrote. More importantly, however, it framed the cultural foundation of his leadership of the company and pointed to what it would become.[45] During DTH's visit to South Africa in 1992, the company spent five weeks traveling around the country, hosting workshops and collaborations with dancers to share DTH's dance tradition and to learn from theirs. Following the company's renaissance in 2013, Naidu would initiate a similar partnership with the Cameroon National Ballet, providing opportunities for dance exchange between both Cameroon and DTH dancers in Yaoundé and New York. A South African who graduated from the University of Cape Town Ballet School, Naidu reflected on the enormous honor he felt to be among those performing for South Africa's first black president. "For a South African artist like me," Naidu said, "few moments compare to the deep honor and reverence I felt that night."

Naidu's story is a quintessential Story of Self, the foundational story of public leadership. In the story of Self, a brand leader must reflect the source of their own calling and the choices that have shaped their personal history. Standing on stage in front of Nelson Mandela as a symbol of a new era in race relations in South Africa was a moment not wholly of Naidu's making, but one that as a South African held unique importance. What's more, that experience planted the seed that became the future vision of what DTH became under his leadership.

According to Ganz, the challenge, the choice, and the outcome conspire to teach us a moral lesson.[46] "When we tell a story," Ganz says, "we enable the listener to enter its time and place with us, see what we see, hear what we hear, feel what we feel." The last line of Naidu's story beautifully summarizes his moral lesson:

*With a more subtle common understanding of the world, its cultures, and its identities enabled by performance art, people can come together more quickly to solve problems, find solutions, and build common cause.*

There is no shortage of reasons *why* mission-driven brand leaders should embrace the opportunity to use stories to convey brand messages. Ultimately, good storytelling brings good work to life. But telling stories well requires structure and forethought.

While we had initially started *The New Global Citizen* as a channel for PYXERA Global's stories, it quickly became a portal for other like-minded changemakers. Helping Laveen Naidu tell his moving story helped me realize how many people have remarkable experiences bottled up inside that either no one has asked to hear, or the would-be storyteller lacks the tools to share through traditional means. At the end of this chapter, I outline the seven steps that can help storytellers more capably convey their stories of impact. The enthusiasm with which people responded to the steps showcased how, given the tools, anyone can become an effective storyteller. Again and again, the seven steps provided people intimidated by the prospect of storytelling with the structure they needed to find the right words in the correct order.

Of course, it is not only organizational leaders who deserve to tell stories and have their stories told. Those who can most significantly expand a brand's influence and reputation often have the least amount of voice: namely the people who benefit from the cause. While finding and developing beneficiary stories can sometimes be expensive and challenging work, it pays off. Research conducted by Adam Grant and his team at the University of Pennsylvania demonstrated how beneficiary interaction influenced the effectiveness of university fundraisers. The results are impressive and dramatic.[47] "Even minimal, brief contact with beneficiaries can enable employees to maintain their motivation," the researchers write in their report.[48] Empowering people to share how your brand has shaped their life has a twofold benefit: encouraging someone to share a personal story increases that individual's commitment to the brand, while also simultaneously offering inspiration to others.

## The Story of Us

The Story of Us takes the Story of Self into community. It asks the public narrator—whether a brand or its leader—to convey the shared motivating values and experiences of a community, and to express a vision of a shared future. In this way, the values and vision of a brand come to life for the brand audience. Who is the "Us" that will be unified to achieve this mission, to do this work? Whereas personal choices often drive the Story of Self, the Story of Us often draws on collective experience. The simplest examples are found in common age and origin—the same graduating class, generation, or hometown. Sometimes, however, the "we" in question originates from an unexpected shared connection.

You might wonder how I wound up traversing a flash flood in Dakar, Senegal. A few hours earlier, I had sat on an old faded couch munching a falafel sandwich, surveying my surroundings with equal parts wonder and joy. Apart from myself and one other, the room was filled with Peace Corps volunteers. I marveled at how, in less than twenty-four hours, I had found my way from an aisle seat on South African Airways to a room full of people I had never before met.

A woman I met with earlier that afternoon had introduced me to a local Peace Corps volunteer who she believed could support the project. This exchange at 3:30 was quickly followed by a phone call. The volunteer advised that she would be leaving the city the next day and would not return until late evening, three days later. She was, however, happy for me to come over to her apartment to discuss the project and join her and a few others for dinner. It was this unexpected exchange that led me to the falafel sandwich on the faded couch.

After the meal, the group headed out to a 9-o'clock movie. It had rained a great deal that afternoon, and close to six inches of water had flooded the streets. Another volunteer took out her phone to light the way, and we followed single file along the least-damp stretch of road, eventually hopping across pieces of cinder block placed to form a path above the flood.

As I followed their lead, just barely able to make out the next cinder block ahead, I pondered the chain of unanticipated moments that had brought me to be hopping across floodwaters in Africa. I found myself both pleased and surprised by the mysterious web life weaves. Life often feels like hopping from stone to stone in the midst of a great flood, as we each try to get from one place to the next. All the better if we can share meals, advice, and partnerships along the way.

Ganz emphasizes that the Story of Us not only helps clarify the guiding values of those belonging to a collective identity, but also provides key unity markers. "Stories then not only teach us how to live," Ganz says, "but also teach us how to distinguish who 'we' are from 'others,' reducing uncertainty about what to expect from our community."[49]

I scribbled the experience that had taken place over the past twenty-four hours into a notebook as I lay awake in bed that night, and I awoke early to submit the story for publication before beginning a full day of project-scoping meetings. The story was not a strategic piece of thought leadership for PYXERA Global, but it was an expression of the unifying qualities of those who set out to do good in the world. Those who invite one another to dinner with little pretense are the same as those who look out for one another along the way. Indeed, the pursuit of mission-driven work can feel a great deal like hopping from cinder block to cinder block in the dark, with only the dim glow of a cell phone to light your way.

## The Story of Now

The Story of Now calls on a community to take action in the face of an urgent challenge ahead, and clarifies the actions required to achieve its vision. Whereas the Stories of Self and Us are self-aware and reflective, the Story of Now is an aspirational call to action, one that can empower a community to overcome obstacles of alienation, isolation, and fear, to emerge enthusiastic, engaged, and ready to collaborate.

"A story of now," Ganz says, "articulates an urgent challenge—or threat—to the values that we share that demand action now. What choice must we make? What is at risk? And where's the hope? In a Story of Now, we are the protagonists, and it is our choices that shape the outcome."[50]

While the Story of Self may be a long-form arc that takes shape over a lifetime, the Stories of Us and Now are often shifting and transient, reframed by new events and experiences. The brand leader's ability to tell the most inspiring version of each is critical to creating a public narrative powerful enough to drive change.

*The New Global Citizen* began as a brand-centered storytelling platform, one distant enough from CDC Development Solutions to stand on its own, yet close enough to PYXERA Global to advance the same essential mission. While the magazine emphasized the stories related to PYXERA Global's practice areas, Deirdre White often published pieces outlining her vision for a better world, framing the Now confronting the global development community. Deirdre unapologetically issued frequent calls to action, invoking others to share her commitment to big, systemic transformation. The Sustainable Development Goals (SDGs) became an anchor point, a shared moment that offered the chance to make big change.

In 2014, White encouraged development leaders to champion three things: data collection and analysis, documentation and replication, and systematic approaches to a few key challenges.[51] She called on the development community to find "New Words, Better Ideas, & Dramatic Innovation to Build a Better World."[52] She fiercely questioned the dominant narrative, whether it was seventeen SDGs or the new vocabulary of "shared value."[53]

Ganz analyzed the ways that Barack Obama and his 2008 campaign leveraged the Stories of Self, Us, and Now to motivate the energy that became a unified vision of #yeswecan.[54] "Through public narrative," Ganz instructs, "leaders—and participants—can move to action by mobilizing sources of motivation, constructing new shared individual and collective identities, and finding the courage to act."[55] In 2016, Ganz and his coauthor Hahrie Han once again analyzed the rhetoric of presidential candidates, analyzing how both Bernie

Sanders and Donald Trump leveraged public narrative to mobilize their bases in ways that eluded Hillary Clinton.[56] Ganz emphasizes that "stories, strategically told, can powerfully rouse a sense of urgency; hope; anger; solidarity; and the belief that individuals, acting in concert, can make a difference."[57]

By identifying the brand's storytellers, and discovering the Stories of Self, Us, and Now that most need to be told, a brand can use its story strategy to attract the right community of brand advocates. In this way, a brand's stories build an important bridge from the brand foundations into the next sequence of steps, brand activation: the curation of experience, community, and action.

## Seven Steps to Stories That Stick

Storytelling is both an art and a science, a unique combination of personal style and structured delivery. These seven steps provide the guidance and structure novice writers need to tell meaningful stories of impact that will inspire their advocates:

1. **Make a Connection:** The setup for a good story almost always begins with an anecdote or a personal interaction related to the story's subject. Sometimes this is the description of sensation or a provocative quote. Other times it is the narrated setting of your story's protagonist. Naidu's story starts

with the opening of the Civic Theatre performance, a significant moment in time to ground the story for the reader and its author. Starting personal places your readers in the shoes of the subject, to help them imagine the reality you are trying to narrate or explain. Starting personal can help "hook" the readers and draw them into the story.

2. **Sketch the Context:** When you begin a story with an anecdote, you have to provide your readers with immediate context about where or why the interaction took place. This can mean explaining who is talking and where it happened. My story of the world of cultural exchange starts with me eating a falafel sandwich on a couch, which is then contextualized by my being in Senegal to scope a larger project. Sketching the context around the interaction, rather than around the subject of the piece as a whole, once again helps bring the reader into your experience.

3. **Provide a Backdrop:** Once you have provided immediate context for the action taking place among the players in your story, it is important to turn to the broader historical backdrop to the action, including where it is happening and why you or your subject is so engaged. Such background can be conveyed in general terms, or, ideally, as the witnessed experience of the author.

4. **Frame the Challenge:** With only a hero and a happy ending, a story has no arc. The hurdle— or challenge—provides a story with tension that engages the curiosity of the listener to wonder: how will this story end? The hurdle can be a problem that affects your story's subject specifically, or a widespread challenge that your protagonist seeks to address. Provide as much detail as you can about the challenge and its origins without turning your story into an academic missive on the subject. While the balance can be a challenge, be sure to focus on the key details that are relevant to your thesis and the point your story is trying to reinforce. Appropriately framing the challenge is especially important for the Story of Now.

5. **Present a Solution:** Simply articulating a challenge will leave your listener feeling frustrated. To leave your reader feeling inspired and hopeful, you have to present the problem's solution, whether it is only being tested, is already in widespread use, or is simply developed in theory. At the highest level, your explanation of the solution should chart the hypothetical or planned course ahead to address the problems you have presented. By outlining potential solutions to the challenge(s) you have introduced, you also create the opportunity to keep your readers engaged, helping them see how they can play a role in what will happen next.

6. **Bring it Full Circle:** The very best stories return to the setup introduced in the story's first lines. What role did those individuals play in executing the solution? How will this result affect their lives? Bringing your readers back to the initial human connection is especially important when narrating a story of mission and impact.

7. **Always Have the Last Word:** Online content is growing at an exponential rate and many writers have realized that most online readers are fickle at best—fewer than half of those who see a story will get halfway through reading it. Yet the last line of your story is nonetheless crucial, leaving your readers with the final message you want them to remember. Perhaps it is a moral or a call to action. Whatever it may be, craft your last words with care.

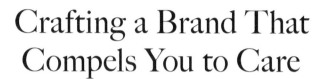

## CHAPTER 7

# Crafting a Brand That Compels You to Care

*Believe in love. Believe in magic. Hell, believe in Santa Claus. Believe in others. Believe in yourself. Believe in your dreams. If you don't, who will?*
—Jon Bon Jovi

"I believe—"

The words rang out over the assembled crowd, a lone voice summoning those gathered before him.

"I believe!" echoed back, multiplied a thousand-fold.

"I believe that—"

Again, the booming echo swelled.

"I believe that she will win!"

This time the response echoed not once, but again and again, accompanied by clapping hands and stomping feet, until the speed of repetition became too fast to sustain and the room erupted into one giant full-throated cheer.

In the first days of my time working to elect Hillary Clinton as "the next president of the United States," the campaign convened its entire team from across the state of Florida for two days of training. Part rally, part boot camp, the two days were designed to boost both accountability and morale.

The local paper reported that the candidate had donor visits planned in the same city at the same time, and all of us whispered hopefully about an impending surprise appearance. However, by the afternoon of the second day, it was evident she was not coming to meet with us. We would have to satisfy ourselves with alternative inspiration.

A three-minute video would have to do the trick. A mash-up of the candidate herself and her surrogates waving and pounding fists on podiums—at the Democratic National Convention, at rallies, at speeches—their words of inspiration scrolled across the screen in typeface to compensate for the ear-splitting (and uplifting) screams and cheers the video would surely elicit.

The hotel ballroom overflowed with people who had come from across the United States to give everything they had and more to this candidate and her campaign. A culture of unity is critical to the success of any effort, but here in the campaign homestretch to Get Out the Vote, this group of humans would be asked to work harder than they had ever done before. The video and the subsequent chant (We-believe-that-she-will-win! We-believe-that-she-will-win!) were meant to bond us together, to make us a united front connected by our forthcoming blood, sweat, and tears, and, of course, our deep-seated shared belief.

Tears streamed down my face as I whooped at full volume and clapped my hands. Such moments are an experience, a shared moment that turns strangers into allies, converting a disaggregated collection of separate individuals into a unified whole.

As an experienced event producer, I understood with perfect clarity the result our training team was working to achieve, even as I was overcome by its effect. I looked around the room, imprinting the moment in my memory. While I had never worked such a large group of people into such a lather with a three-minute video, I had experience shaping moments in time for dramatic effect.

## What Makes Brand Experiences So Powerful?

Brand experience—the moment of direct connection between a person and a brand—is formative. That interaction can deeply affect both the individual and their relationship with the brand. When you visit someplace new, you witness how your firsthand experience of a new place can transform your perspective. For brands, experiences offer the opportunity to curate moments in time that can foster conversion in mindset and catalyze a commitment to take action on a brand's behalf.

Beyond all of the details of what makes a terrific event, brand experience is a solidification of ritual that will define the community it creates. Rituals manifest in many different ways: how you cook your food; how you wake up or go to sleep; the sayings you use to explain certain feelings or emotions. When you bring people together in support of a brand, you have the chance to ritualize how people engage with one another. Research suggests that rituals can change people's state of mind, influencing their feelings and demeanor.[58] More importantly, perhaps, people do not have to believe in the ritual's power for it to change their behavior. According to Francesca Gina and Michael Norton, "Despite the absence of a direct causal connection between the ritual and the desired outcome, performing rituals with the intention of producing a certain result appears to be sufficient for that result to come true." Gina and Norton claim that, "While some rituals are unlikely to be effective—knocking on wood will not bring rain—many everyday rituals make a lot of sense and are surprisingly effective," most notably, those surrounding loss and grief.[59]

Further, positive emotions have a high degree of sociability. This means that you are more likely to experience joy and euphoria in a community of like-minded individuals than sitting alone on your living-room couch. Human beings seek the community of others in order to feel a different kind of happiness. According to Nigel Barber, "We are not incapable of being happy when alone, of course, but there is a specific type of happiness that is induced by group interactions."[60]

It may seem obvious, but research has shown that modeled behavior is a primary mode of human learning.[61] What a person sees shapes both what they do and what they believe to be possible. As such, brand experience has the potential to not only disseminate information to your audience, but show them the action you expect them to take in the future. In this sense, the medium becomes the message. By capitalizing on the overwhelmingly positive emotions people experience in the community of their peers, you can reinforce the positive effects of your brand's rituals, to foster your community's commitment to sustained action now and in the future.

## A Brand Experience is a Production

My first production opportunity presented itself during my sophomore year in college, when a friend invited me to join her as the producer of *The Laramie Project*. The play chronicles the events surrounding the murder of Matthew Shepard, a gay student at the University of Wyoming killed in a hate crime. A talented creative team conceived of and executed a masterful piece of theatre. Thirty onstage television sets of a wide range of shapes and sizes mimicked the media circus that descended on Laramie, Wyoming, following Matthew Shepard's heinous murder in 1998. (This was 2005, before everyone carried a video camera in their back pocket.) My work on *The Laramie Project* ignited my passion for production. Early in my career, I realized that the same dynamics at play in a theatre production are also relevant in a professional setting.

Fast forward to 2009, when I found myself in an industry dominated by dramatic effect. Through a series of unlikely events, I had become the director of development at the Institute for the Study of War (ISW), a national-security think tank in Washington, DC, an organization whose values were not wholly aligned with my own. In a challenging economic environment, I embraced the professional opportunity that had presented itself. After being hired as a development associate, I was soon assigned the duties of development manager, and shortly thereafter, development director. My mission was simple: expand the organization's donor base and operating budget. Over the course of the next eighteen months, our team planned and executed numerous fundraisers and events, ultimately undertaking a half-million-dollar campaign to launch a new Middle East Security Project that offered research and analysis on the implications of the Arab Spring of 2011.

Then, the big kahuna. On July 18, 2011, General David Petraeus announced his retirement from the US Army. The very same day, ISW's president called our team from Afghanistan: we had two and a half weeks to plan a gala dinner for the general, celebrating his return home. Over the course of the previous year, the organization's president had spent a considerable amount of time in the Middle East, advising the US military on their counterinsurgency strategy. Our team had always spoken wistfully of the possibility of hosting General Petraeus for the ultimate donor-cultivation event, and now, without warning, our dreams were coming true.

I had never planned an honorary gala for such a high-profile individual before, much less in such an insanely short time frame, but our team got to work. We hired an event planner to manage the banquet details—tablecloths, place cards, flower arrangements, food selections—and set to work recruiting a room full of prospects. An invitation to a gala for a popular and well-known military commander who has just returned from a year at war is almost guaranteed to be accepted. The challenge was filling the room with the right people and planning the program to drive action appropriately. What favor would each guest receive? What award would we give the general? Who would sit with whom? How would we ensure the program was both intellectually satisfying and entertaining? Each decision and corresponding action had to be completed in less than three weeks.

Light, sound, ambiance, and onstage talent were just as much in play as they had been in *The Laramie Project* six years earlier. Added to these considerations was the challenge of the interaction of our audience with our honored guest, and among themselves. We needed to ensure each attendee enjoyed their conversation and their meal, and walked away feeling a part of the ISW family.

In spite of the compressed timeline, the gala was an enormous success. More than 150 people accepted the invitation, and all but one made it to the dinner. We successfully solicited a corporate sponsorship for the event, covering our costs, and ultimately cultivating many of the people in attendance to support the Middle East Security Project campaign. Two months later, we would celebrate the campaign's success with a field report from another well-known four-star general, General James Mattis.

Often event planners approach special occasions with a lot of lead time, planning incrementally for months and months. A seeming luxury, time can also breed turbulence and second-guesses. Blessedly, the Petraeus gala timeline left us with perfect clarity and conviction on how to proceed, making the process, while stressful, imminently straightforward. We knew exactly what we needed to do and how to do it. Experience design, the process of crafting a user's journey, benefits tremendously from this kind of clarity. [62]

My next big event-planning bonanza would not find me until a few years later when I would have the opportunity to plan an inspiring event under a more realistic timeline. By the spring of 2014, PYXERA Global was six months into a successful brand launch and anticipating another landmark, the celebration of its twenty-fifth anniversary. As part of the rebranding process, PYXERA Global had developed a clear sense of the role it wanted to play in the world. The new mission and vision aligned with the UN Sustainable Development Goals (SDGs), a new framework seeking to inspire organizations in the public, private, and social sectors to align their efforts for maximum impact. The launch of the SDGs coincided with PYXERA Global's twenty-fifth anniversary, a coincidence that inspired the inaugural Global Engagement Forum in November 2015.

PYXERA Global was well-poised to take advantage of the moment and explicitly link its new focus on linking partnership among the public, private, and social sectors with purposeful global engagement and the SDGs. The

Global Engagement Forum would build on the success of past events, convening leaders from Fortune 500 companies alongside representatives from the US government and leading nonprofits for a two-day experience focused on how trisector partnership could make a difference in advancing the SDGs.

Six years earlier, PYXERA Global had begun hosting an annual conference focused specifically on the emerging discipline of corporate volunteering in emerging markets. When I joined the organization, I involved myself in the planning process for the 2013 conference, ultimately taking the lead role in onstage production. The conference was a day and a half of panels, TED-style talks, and breakout sessions. In 2014, the vision for the conference expanded to include a three-hour live broadcast. The Public-Private Partnership Forum, which featured five conversations focused on business, education, health, corporate diplomacy, and partnership, was streamed live from the Knight Studio at the Newseum, one of Washington, DC's marquee production spaces. [63] Between that first year and the next, sponsorship doubled as companies such as SAP, the Dow Chemical Company, Merck, and others began to embrace greater involvement and visibility in global development.

Building on this success, we programmed 2015 as an anniversary year, curating ten months of programming leading up to the first Global Engagement Forum in November. PYXERA Global decided to focus on 10 SDGs.[64] Between January and October, ten webcasts explored a different theme, providing direct links with the role of the private sector and cross-sector collaboration. Twitter chats created a visible dialogue between key players in the domains of health and water. Rather than simply focusing our annual event on one side of PYXERA Global's business—global pro bono—as we had done in the past, we embraced the chance to integrate other practice areas within the organization.

Back when I was planning the Petraeus homecoming gala, time constraints made our objective crystal clear: we had twenty-one days to convene 150 prospective donors. Successful events are often iterative. Our ability to plan and produce a gala in three weeks was aided by our having produced similar events before. We had existing guest lists to invite to attend and a roster of corporate partners to invite to sponsor. We had laid the groundwork, a community of support, that made the tight timeline workable. When planning PYXERA Global's twenty-fifth-anniversary celebration and the first Global Engagement Forum, we had the luxury of more time to plan, but the same foundation held. The Global Engagement Forum built on past conferences and a well-established list of regular attendees. The willingness to expand the event's vision to address a broader objective was partly due to the timing—the twenty-fifth anniversary coinciding with the launch of the SDGs—but also confidence bolstered by past success.

No matter the timeline, both feasibility and objectivity are vital to producing a successful and impactful experience. A team must define what it will prioritize and how it will measure success. Using the reference of past experience, a task list emerges with appropriate deadlines. In the case of the Petraeus homecoming, each day that followed was filled with tasks that had to be completed within forty-eight hours. In the case of PYXERA Global's twenty-fifth-anniversary celebration, our challenge was to plan out the actions we would take over the course of an entire year.

Then, of course, there was the event itself, the unifying experience with the potential to catalyze a change in mindset and commitment among those convened. The Newseum provided a premium venue. Each session was coached in advance, ensuring that the moderator clearly understood the questions to be asked of each speaker, and the broader idea to be amplified. For each TED-style talk, speakers rehearsed multiple times in advance to ensure their talks were memorized and seamless. Breakout sessions were primed to provide opportunities for meaningful hands-on engagement and learning. We hosted a gala dinner in Union Station's East Hall. As a landmark event, every detail mattered. By every measure, PYXERA Global's 25th Anniversary celebration and the first Global Engagement Forum were a huge success.

## TED and Ideas Worth Spreading

During my time in Washington, DC, I had attended dozens of events which varied widely in scope and scale: gala dinners at the posh Mandarin Oriental, live broadcasts at the highbrow Brookings Institution, conferences at the Grand Hyatt and the JW Marriott, and roundtable discussions at the National Press Club. Nothing, however, provided stronger event inspiration for me than TED.

I clearly recall the first TED talk I ever watched: Sheryl Sandberg's TEDWomen presentation of the prelude to *Lean In*. I was awestruck by the rigorous coaching and preparation—invisible to the audience—that positioned each speaker as the ultimate expert in their domain. The extraordinarily high level of production ensured the video was a joy to watch afterward.

Of course, by 2010 I was already late to the game. TED had already been in existence for more than two decades. Just a few years earlier, TED had launched TEDx, a licensing program that allowed communities and universities to host TED events of their own. This expansion helped TED become a mainstream social influencer, a multimedia Reddit of sorts, which helped to upvote high-powered ideas into the broader human consciousness. While TED began specifically focused on "technology, entertainment, and design," it quickly evolved beyond these constraints to provide a platform for all manner of "ideas worth spreading."

Just six months after the 2015 Global Engagement Forum, I stumbled into an opportunity to produce a TED event of my own. A group of professionals in Tysons Corner, Virginia was in the process of planning their inaugural event. Speakers and venue had been selected, and at least 100 people were slated to attend. Unfortunately, none of the founders had experience overseeing a live stage production. Initially recruited to manage the audiovisual team, I realized the gap in the team's production experience and stepped in as the producer and stage manager, hosting pre-show coordination calls with speakers, organizing the tech crew, and managing the minute-to-minute flow of production the day of the show. With just two months from when I joined the team to the actual production date, it was a whirlwind of action, but ultimately an enormous success.

Regardless of the amount of lead time permitted, managing several key factors can ensure that you produce an effective and inspiring brand experience.

1. **Objective Clarity:** Dynamic events require high-level inspiration and oversight. What is the primary goal you are trying to achieve and how will this high-level brand experience help you move toward that outcome? When it's over, how will you judge success? The best events

use a three-pronged strategy: to entertain, to educate, and to motivate. Research has shown that laughter can generate dopamine and endorphins, prompting people to remember an experience better. Ensuring your event is entertaining will take advantage of this fact.[65] Most mission-driven events have some educational purpose, and it is important to clarify exactly what you want different segments of your audience to learn from their experience well in advance. Lastly, a well-crafted event will motivate an audience to want to take action on behalf of the brand. Providing opportunities for your audience to embody and act on that motivation during the event will ensure they carry it forward into their everyday lives. By clarifying these high-level objectives up front, you can ensure your event will advance your brand and achieve your goals.

2. **Pre-Planning & Coordination:** Multiday events must provide tailored experiences for specific segments of your audience. Once the key themes are defined, these points of focus must be messaged effectively and reiterated throughout the program. Speakers and moderators need coaching and support to ensure they deliver the right message to the audience. Coaching meetings familiarize onstage talent with the production set-up they will encounter on the day of the event. It is risky to

assume anyone knows what you want of them on the day of the performance. Taking the time to plan your work and work your plan, when it comes to event execution, will ensure all of the details align. All participants must understand with clarity the role they play in achieving your high-level objectives.

3. **Onstage Production:** Every live production has a lights-camera-action moment. For recurring theatre productions, you usually get at least one dress rehearsal to get it wrong. However, for conferences and other brand experiences, you often only get one chance to get it right. This circumstance means that some of your speakers will wilt in the moment and others will naturally be on point. It is up to the production team to do everything they can to help that person shine. Lighting, sound, and special effects drive the ambiance and your speaker's comfort. When a speaker walks onstage and winces at how bright the lights are or taps a microphone to test that it is working, you are interrupting the flow of energy from your speaker to your audience. The run of show, a theatre mainstay, provides critical structure and guidance, specifying every action and the target minute of run time when it should be completed, keeping the expectations of every single production team member aligned.

4. **Audience Experience:** Masters of high-quality production ensure that events both inspire and motivate. Keeping the audience engaged and motivated requires not just informative sessions, but fun! There is nothing like a dance break or a seventh-inning stretch to liven up an event. Music, stretching, and call-and-response activities can help get an audience excited and keep them engaged. Breakouts and workshops are as important to a successful event as keynotes and entertainment. This element of the programming, too, must serve each segment of the audience with sessions that are engaging, informative, and inspiring.

5. **The Wisdom in the Room:** Tim Brown said it first: "All of us are smarter than any of us."[66] For decades (and maybe even centuries), experts on stage have defined the structure and substance of events, but in recent years, the knowledge of those present has begun to gain traction. The unconference, an event format in which groups crowdsource session topics and facilitators, has become increasingly popular, taking advantage of the specific experience of those who attend. Production teams must provide the structure and support to help people connect with like-minded collaborators, learn from one another, and take action. In these cases, programming that leverages the talent in the

room can enhance the enjoyment and inspiration of everyone present.

6. **Assess Your Impact:** Know what your audience is thinking? Do you have a plan to find out? Before, during, and after an event, it is critical to assess how people are receiving the experience you are curating. Pre- and post-event assessment methods can help you both understand how successful your event was, and what after-action steps are required to support your audience in taking action.

When it comes to brand experience, flexibility and adaptability are critical. As you seek to build the foundation of brand activation, it is important to be attentive to who shows up and the issues that arise. Most of all, you must keep an eye on the future. You can measure an event's success by how well it fosters community and action, which requires its own intentional design and curation.

## CHAPTER 8

# Unleashing the Power of Community

*"The greatness of a community is most accurately measured by the compassionate actions of its members."*
—Coretta Scott King

"People like us do things like this."

I always knew Seth Godin was a genius, but the first time I heard him speak live, he floored me with the simplicity of his clarity: people like us do things like this.

He meant that the world quite easily divides itself into in-groups and out-groups, differentiated by shared practice. When you are trying to market something to someone, you have to know who the "us" in "people like us" is, or no one will listen. You have to understand how to document and replicate "things like this."

Seth was giving a keynote talk at the 2017 StartingBloc Institute in New York, the five-day initiation experience for StartingBloc, one of the most powerful communities ever conceived. StartingBloc is a fellowship of more than 3,000 changemakers who believe in heartfelt leadership and who individually and collectively take responsibility for shifting the culture of the world toward regenerative, socially conscious, sustainable systems—one project, department, or company at a time. That room of more than 100 incoming StartingBloc Fellows was a remarkably well-defined group of "people like us," brought together in one time and place.

Research and experience have demonstrated that community, while sometimes amorphous and hard to curate, is defined by five essential factors: people, purpose, practice, place, and progress. The first two go hand in hand. "People like us" are those united by their shared purpose. The trick is to figure out what will compel people to reveal their common cause to one another, to raise their hand and say, "Yes, I'm in!"

## Building Community Through Connection

The first three steps—ideology, identity, and message— provide the foundations from which to communicate. The fourth and fifth—story and experience—amplify a brand outward, and invite advocates to connect with the brand and one another. Moving into the last two steps of the Heptagon Method—community and action—the transition from one step to the next paves a pathway toward progress and impact. Football offers an apt point of reference. A team's head coach and the quarterback, leaders both on and off the field, define the ideology and set the tone for how the team operates and communicates. (Ask any football fan to describe the difference between the values of Bill Belichick and Tom Brady of the New England Patriots versus Mike McCarthy and Aaron Rodgers of the Green Bay Packers). The audience for each team is often clearly defined—by geography and a team's unique history. So-called "Mass-holes" (New England Patriots fans) are a different breed from the ever-hopeful fans of the "Cleveland Frowns." The endless riff of derogatory nicknames ensures that every fan has ammunition to lob at their opponents (message). In the National Football League (NFL), rivalries run deep, and the league takes clear advantage of their differences in how it designs a season. The sequencing of a team's schedule defines how it communicates—the story it tells—while the games themselves—both on TV and in the stadium—offer unique brand experiences that are prescheduled many months in advance. Each team spends millions of dollars on a curated brand arc, and it pays off. Die-hard fans spend money on tickets and DIRECTV subscriptions, year after year, to feel connected to their allies.

Sports fans are among the most visible examples of well-formed communities that expand and persist in the midst of modern life. Their purpose is singular—to cheer for their team, win or lose. While the practices of any specific sports fan might vary, the most important is obvious: showing up in team colors on game day. On Sundays in the fall, bars across America fill with women and men in the jerseys of their favorite players, to "coach" every play. Still more fans huddle at home, often watching multiple games simultaneously on different screens. Any media expert will tell you, in the months of September through January, "The NFL owns Sunday."

Avid football fans have another parallel practice. "Tailgating," which was once only a traffic violation, has now become a ubiquitous pregame practice in which fans gather outside of stadiums hours before game time to barbeque, eat, and drink. "Pregaming" has now emerged as a widely used euphemism for early drinking in any context. Both practices have a specific connection to place. Tailgating takes place in the parking lot outside the arena. Pregaming takes place at home. These joyful practices present place-based moments of unity and solidarity. However, not every successful community has such an obvious unifying livery and tradition of public celebration. Two powerful communities have deeply shaped my adult life.

In 2015, I stumbled into an extraordinarily well-formed community, entirely by accident. I went to my first yoga class at age thirteen. In my adulthood, yoga quickly became my primary mode of exercise. In 2015, I set out looking for a new physical experience and found that my regular yoga studio offered an acroyoga fundamentals class. I decided to check it out. The class began with everyone seated in a circle, each person sharing a response to a reflection question. What's your favorite flower? What are you most excited about? I had previously known yoga to be a fundamentally individual experience—me on a mat doing my own thing. Acroyoga, I discovered, is a highly collaborative activity. Combining the practices of yoga, acrobatics, and Thai massage, acroyoga (acrobatic yoga) challenges its practitioners to explore yoga poses balanced on the feet or hands of a partner.[67] A progression of poses followed a physical warm-up activity.

After they grow too heavy for "airplane" as a child, few adults get to experience the exhilaration of flight. To the uninitiated observer, acroyoga looks difficult and dangerous. With good alignment and support, however, most beginners can learn a series of intermediate poses with relative ease. Having spent the better part of the previous twenty years with my feet or hands firmly planted on my mat, after just one thrilling class, I was hooked. Still, it took me time to learn the unique practices of this community.

Acroyoga is not well-suited to the indoor clearance of modern construction. Most indoor spaces have low ceilings that make stacking human bodies two high impractical. As a result, in warm weather, many acroyogis migrate outdoors.

If you wander around a park in almost any city on a nice spring day, you will find clusters of humans in a shaded and dry corner of the park, balancing on one another's feet and hands. Called "jams," such gatherings emerge seemingly without planning and continue for hours on end. One practitioner approaches another and asks, "Wanna fly?" or "Wanna base?" The flyer takes the hand of the base and gently helps lower the base to the ground. After a series of calibrating poses, which help both people to understand the other's strength and experience, the pair begins to flow from one pose to another.

As a preternaturally type-A human, I found the notion of "jamming" foreign. I was accustomed to showing up for prescheduled classes or meetings in which one person was in charge and the rest listened, asked questions, offered opinions, and left. Mostly these activities were conducted sitting in chairs around a long table, or, as in the case of yoga, with each person on their own mat. I expected it to be awkward, showing up in a public park and asking a stranger to offer their feet. I imagined it might feel like a middle-school dance, everyone sitting around awkwardly, waiting with dread to see who would be picked last (or not at all).

I spent the better part of eight months attending the weekly fundamentals class, gaining strength and confidence with each passing week. In April 2016, I decided I was ready to take my practice to the next level, and I signed up for a weeklong acroyoga festival in Treasure

Beach, Jamaica. In my fundamentals class in Washington, DC, I had become one of the more intermediate practitioners, but in Treasure Beach, surrounded by teachers and experts, I felt like a rookie. Walking into a jam on the first night, I was anxious I would be laughed out of the room. But the culture of acroyoga is kind and collaborative—you cannot learn to fly sitting by yourself in a corner. Experienced acroyogis know that one learns the practice by transference: a novice flying on the hands of a veteran will learn how to give and take energy and weight, just as an inexperienced base will best learn how to move their feet and hands working with a seasoned flyer.

On my third evening in Treasure Beach, I was sitting on a large foam mat in the middle of an outdoor pavilion, waiting for someone to bring the meeting to order when someone approached me from behind, tapped my shoulder and asked, "Do you want to fly?" I had spent the past two days in an elemental immersion, shoring up my knowledge of foundational poses. I had yet to attempt anything overly complicated, so with some trepidation, I said yes. My new friend Guillermo showed me how much I could learn working with someone with a lot more strength and experience. Within the hour, I was moving through flow sequences (called washing machines) I never would have attempted on my own, and I was managing difficult balancing poses with ease.

After my return home from Jamaica, my life quickly took a turn in a different direction. In June, I moved from Washington, DC to New York, and in August, I left PYX-ERA Global to join the Clinton campaign. A year had passed before I found myself in a New York park looking for other acroyogis.[68] Soon, I was flying with a base who minutes before had been a complete stranger.

Acroyoga is not a professional group or an industry but rather an organic practice, a habit of movement, a way of being in the world. Yet it still depends on the five pillars of community: people, purpose, practice, place, and progress. Its people are those who are physically curious, who are seeking a deeper connection with the world around them and with their own bodies. Acroyogis practice giving and receiving extraordinary exertion (acrobatics) and exceptional rejuvenation (Thai massage), with the mutual support of active spotters who keep everyone safe. Their place is as flexible as they are: a soft patch of grass or a shallow body of water, where people can safely stack two high. Each pair measures their progress in the tiny victories and quantum leaps they experience in their practice together.

I never anticipated acroyoga would find its way into this book, but the power of its community has significantly shaped my life and how I think of developing community in my work. In a way, diving into acroyoga helped me see the need for other meaningful professional communities in my life and the way that unusual habits can provide a foundation for sustained connection and commitment.

Though I had no idea when, I knew from my first introduction to StartingBloc I would attend its five-day Institute. A friend and former colleague had participated in an Institute in 2012 and had raved about her experience. I filed it away for the future. An exceptional fundraising consultant who taught me much of what I know about fundraising always cautioned that the choices you make the first time you do something are critical.[69] Once you do it one way, you create an expectation, a confirmation bias you will struggle to overcome. When I set out to launch my own company, I knew I wanted to support and invest in my professional development. Instead of signing up for a random multiweek course, I decided that the intensity of the five-day StartingBloc Institute (which takes place over a weekend) would be most feasible. I had no idea the richness of experience and community that lay ahead.

Part social-impact incubator, part leadership academy, I expected that the StartingBloc Institute would help support my professional development as a new CEO. A few weeks before the Institute, I connected with my breakout group, seven people with whom I would share the five-day immersion. Our mentor had already been through the Institute. At his urging, we scheduled a Google Hangout to "meet" one another before our arrival. At first, the conversation was a little awkward and unsteady, but gradually over the course of the next hour, we began to develop a rapport. Our first task as a group was to name ourselves, a well-known technique for creating allegiance and connection. All of us were excited for the upcoming solar eclipse anticipated during the Institute, and so our identity emerged: Team Eclipse. Entering the Institute with known friends and allies made it seem that much more inviting.

Our mentor created a group chat to help us stay in touch. He encouraged us to arrive a few minutes early to connect in person before the opening session. We stood in a circle, still nearly strangers, but following our mentor's lead, choosing to jump in with both feet and trust one another instead of holding back. "Let's go around the circle and each say what you want out of the Institute," he suggested. Each person said a word that described their hope for the next few days. "Be challenged," I declared. I had no idea exactly what that meant, but there it was.

The next five days are both a blur and a slow-motion newsreel of distinct exchanges that have been powerful in shaping my sense of myself and my future direction. The Institute included inspiring keynote talks from speakers who pushed each of us to imagine our full potential, just as it encourages us to take part in intimate conversations with new friends, designed to uncover formative experiences and personal values. Exercises in human-centered design provided hands-on experience with rapid prototyping and iterative ideation.

The entire multiday adventure fostered a deep connection among all of its participants.

I was indeed challenged, but also deeply supported by the compassionate members of my cohort and the thoughtful mentors who guided our induction into the Fellowship. On the last day, we were invited to offer one another #asks, a clear articulation of what someone needed at that moment in time, and #gives, how a Fellow wanted to support others, establishing the community's culture of open and structured generosity. The organizers also ensured everyone in the group had the chance to express gratitude for the people who had most significantly shaped our experience over the five days. Each of us was invited into a virtual community on Facebook and WhatsApp to keep in touch with the broader StartingBloc community, as well as those in our home city; #asks and #gives would continue within the community's virtual space.

I left StartingBloc unsure of how engaged people would be through these channels but was soon pleased to find them active almost every day. People shared job opportunities alongside declarations of unexpected unemployment and the need for coaching and support. Fellows often hosted events and, more importantly, showed up to support one another in force. Within weeks I had had follow-up coffee chats with close to a dozen Fellows, and by November, I had pitched several new business opportunities that resulted directly from those relationships. Two different

Fellows had taken care of my dog. I had not attended the Institute looking for business-development opportunities, but the strength of the relationships that it forged and the clearly defined purpose of mutual support it fostered guaranteed that Fellows would find ways to help one another, a shining example of the way a rising tide can lift all boats.

## The Psychology of Community

Neither acroyoga nor StartingBloc score full marks on their brand-development arc. Neither has especially well-defined brand foundations nor a robust story strategy. Most people who find their way into acroyoga and StartingBloc do so by happenstance. Once inside, however, the people, purpose, practice, place, and progress are so well-defined that ambitious brand advocates emerge.

In 1986, researchers David McMillan and David Chavis documented a theory that explains the five foundational factors that provide the underpinning for effective communities.[70]

The first pillar of community psychology is membership, the people with whom you will connect and engage. Since in-groups and out-groups inherently define communities, the "people" component of community must have its bounds. A group must clearly convey how people become members and what separates those who are members from those who are not. For acroyoga, this delineation is plain—either you like flying, or you do not. For Starting-Bloc Fellows, the five-day Institute serves as the point of induction for all community members, ensuring that each person has a very similar grounding in their passion for the group. By insisting on clearly defined member-ship criteria, communities foster emotional safety and belonging which in turn encourages members to invest themselves in the community's perpetuation and ex-pansion. Experienced acroyogis willingly teach newbies how to base and fly. In StartingBloc, current Fellows re-turn as mentors who ensure that the values and habits of the group are learned and practiced. Many communities also embrace icons of membership. Sports jerseys, rings, pins, and phrases (#asks & #gives, or "Wanna fly?") are all powerful symbols that define and unite community members.[71]

Unlike school, where people are accustomed to wait-ing for instructions, people show up to a community with a desire to get involved. Effective communities codify their purpose, the second pillar of community, which empowers members to act on its behalf. McMil-lan and Chavis call this "mattering," the symbiotic way in which individual participants infest a group with mutual meaning. This behavior is well-practiced in StartingBloc's tradition of #asks and #gives. Their research finds that "People who acknowledge that others' needs, values, and opinions matter to them are often the most influential group members," meaning that those who give generously of themselves to their community often benefit the most from that behavior. Conversely, "Those who always push to influence, try to dominate others, and ignore the wishes and opinions of others are often the least powerful members."[72] Thus, effective community curation favors rules of engagement that empower members to offer one another support, in service to the greater good.

The third pillar of community is practice, the notion that members must derive some fulfillment from their sustained engagement and involvement with the group. Social media keeps us coming back, day after day, for the gratification of feeling seen. Community benefits need not be monetary or particularly measurable, but community curators must define how they will reward sustainable participation and provide resources that advance the concrete benefit members receive from their generous commitment to support their fellow members and the community's cause.

The fourth pillar of community is place, which instructs how members can meaningfully get involved. Acroyogis consistently find connection on grassy public lawns. StartingBloc Fellows interact regularly on Facebook, WhatsApp, and at quarterly five-day in-person Institutes. Football fans find one another at the tailgate on Sunday afternoon. These practices of place yield stories and mythology that contribute to an enduring historical narrative of the community's power, which changes over time. "Sense of community is not a static feeling," McMillan and Chavis write. "It is affected by time through changing values and external forces such as commerce, the media, transportation, specialization of professions, economics, and employment factors."[73] This historical and present context can define the boundaries of connection, while also encouraging engagement. When we are lonely or fearful, the social fabric of connection can take us in and help us to feel a part of something bigger.

Lastly, communities are anchored in progress. How will this self-defined group of people advance their common cause? Whether that be increasing one person's individual comfort in an especially challenging acroyoga pose or accelerating the movement of society toward greater inclusion and justice, every community must define its own standard of evolution and growth.

The funny thing about communities is you know them when you see them; before they exist, you can easily become discouraged and doubt your ability to spark such a connection. Communities sometimes emerge organically, in the right place and at the right time. Witness the explosion of groups using the Indivisible Guide to engage their elected representatives following the election of Donald Trump. More often than not, however, communities arise because the proper foundations have been laid for them to develop. Having clearly defined purpose—an ideology—is critical; people have to understand why they should participate. Telling stories that inspire the right people to raise their hand and get involved—the stories of Self, Us, and Now—amplifies its purpose. A brand experience convenes people to feel their shared intent, to understand the value of both giving and receiving from the collective. To get started, however, someone has to envision the creation of something where there once was nothing.

In 2017 I had the chance to plant a seed of community myself. A string of circumstances led me to connect with an Italian organization seeking to strengthen their partnership within the United States. LabGov, the Laboratory for the Governance of the Commons, had been working for five years on developing urban-commons projects in Europe. Now they wanted to begin partnering with US cities. Inspired by their work, I helped them submit a proposal to the Rockefeller Foundation's retreat center in Bellagio, Italy, which promised a five-day retreat for up to twenty-two leaders. When we learned the foundation had approved our proposal, we began inviting a diverse group of city leaders who represented cities across the United States, Europe, and elsewhere to join us for a five-day discussion of the future of the city as a commons.

In advance of our arrival, freak snowstorms ripped across Northern Europe and the eastern United States. All but six of the attendees experienced some travel delay; many were delayed by more than twenty-four hours. Our brand experience was off to a rocky start! Yet over the course of four days, over lunches and after-dinner drinks, our group began to cohere, with civil activists learning from municipal leaders and foundation funders offering lessons to corporate leaders and vice versa. On the evening of the last day, we sat around a conference table, discussing how to move forward. What actions would each person take following the return home? When would everyone come together to speak again? We agreed that quarterly phone calls would provide the right cadence of contact.

Three months later, many of those who attended the Bellagio retreat joined the first quarterly call. Two new members of the group, who had not been able to attend the retreat in Bellagio, presented on urban-commons-based projects under development in their cities. A common theme of urban agricultural development emerged. Someone suggested hosting a public webinar on the topic to engage more people interested in the commons. We planned to host our next call in May and reconvene at the We Make the City festival in Amsterdam in June. Later, another member suggested a focus on "learning processes," hosting face-to-face dialogue and internal workshops for members to work on more clearly understanding shared issues and interests. Slowly but surely, the structure of community was beginning to emerge.

Many brands would like to wave a magic wand and instantly have the support of a community of advocates, but the seeds of deep engagement take time to take root. The foundations that allow the community to take shape are quite simple: Identify the right people, clearly define their shared purpose, provide the structure for practice and place, and define their shared standard of progress. With those seeds of connection well planted and watered, your community will flourish.

**The Five Pillars of Community**

- **People:** Who are the "people like us" you will invite to come together?
- **Purpose:** What is the mission and vision you will seek to serve together?
- **Practice:** How will you show up for one another to put your purpose into action?
- **Place:** Where will your people find one another in order to practice?
- **Progress:** How will you measure your success in achieving your purpose?

When the five pillars are present, the alchemy of community is primed to take place. Within the context of brand activation, community is a bridge. It is the container in which brand advocates find common cause. By offering structure to support sustained engagement, your organization creates the foundation to empower your advocates to move to the next and final step: action.

CHAPTER 9

# Inspiring Individuals to Take Action

*"Never doubt that a small group of thoughtful, committed citizens can change the world. Indeed, it is the only thing that ever has."*
—Margaret Mead

In the absence of a broadly held ideology, the Hillary Clinton campaign used another method to motivate its staff and volunteers. Each member of the field team was encouraged and coached to develop a "personal story," the hero's journey that had called us to serve on the campaign. This story would help motivate both volunteers and voters to support the campaign more deeply. In my first few weeks on the campaign, I heard many stories that touched me deeply, stories of health disenfranchisement, of bigotry against my gay and lesbian colleagues. As I searched for my own personal story I was profoundly aware and self-conscious of the ways the extraordinary privilege I had enjoyed throughout my life had allowed me to escape the scarring hurt of so many wrongs others had suffered. If not to secure the Affordable Care Act, or protect the rights of LGBTQ Americans, what had called me here to do this important yet grueling work? The answer was my maternal grandmother: Marjorie.

Born in 1911, Marjorie Tilley Dunbar lived through two world wars and the Great Depression. Her early years of marriage to my grandfather were filled with unusual adventures in pre-WWII Europe. After being caught serving as foreign agents, Marjorie spent months in solitary confinement in a convent. Following her release, she and my grandfather spent the better part of a year moving around Europe on two-week visas, finally landing in Austria. She spoke ominously of watching Hitler's march into Salzburg in 1938, and of their hurried efforts to escape Europe before war broke out. Upon their return, my grandparents settled down in upstate New York. Marjorie became a housewife and mother to four children, as women were wont to do in the 1940s. Then, at age 39, she awoke one morning to find her husband dead on the kitchen floor from a brain aneurysm. Quite suddenly, her world once again shifted.

By the time I got to know my Marjorie, my grandfather's passing was a distant memory in her long and storied life. Marjorie, who lived to 92, went on to remarry happily. She became a 4H leader and served on the town council in her home of Marbletown, New York. There, she became a champion for conservation, helping to rewrite zoning laws that would shape the local development of land for generations.

Moments of catalytic crisis would come to define the course of my grandmother's life. Yet she always managed to remain calm and focused in the face of impending chaos.

"You have to pull up your socks and get on with it," she would say.

Defying circumstance and expectation, she helped me understand in my youth that our lives are what we make of them. Sometimes circumstances that appear to present insurmountable obstacles are only temporary problems awaiting their eventual resolution. I always felt blessed to have the good fortune to know my grandmother, who lived until age 92. She taught me to sew, to cook, and to bake, small acts of creation that I both practice and cherish. More importantly, however, she was a living example of how paralysis prevents progress.

In Chapter 1, I mentioned four big lessons that have shaped my life and career and inform this approach to transform purpose into power. It turns out there is a fifth:

5. *When you are not sure what to do, the important thing is to do something.*

In the summer of 2016, I knew I had to do something about the political challenge facing America. When I quit my job and moved to Florida to join the Florida Democratic Party as a field organizer, my grandmother's urging to pull up my socks and *do something* was ringing in my ears. The months I spent working to elect the first female President of the United States, and my failure to do so, were formative experiences. Both helped me realize how the failure to express a shared purpose can diminish people's motivation to take action.

Motivating your advocates to act on behalf of your brand is the ultimate payoff most mission-driven organizations are working towards, the moment when your constituents exercise their own conviction on behalf of your shared purpose. Often when organizations go out looking for help, it is because the action part isn't working.

"We haven't met our fundraising targets this year. We're worried."

"No one is sharing our content online. Why?"

"Our work depends on the commitment of our volunteers to achieve our goals, but they always no-show at the last minute."

Such problems indicate a deeper issue with how an organization communicates and amplifies its mission.

Effectively using the Heptagon Method means being willing to start at the beginning—with ideology—but it also demands a clear end goal. Typically, an organization must undertake an array of actions to advance its mission which means that the "action" you are working towards can vary based on the circumstance.

## Six Actions That Accelerate Impact

When it comes to "action," a lot of organizations are concerned with how they will achieve their funding goals. This concern is logical. Without a budget, it is hard to do the work. Before setting out to ask people for money, however, organizations need to demonstrate their worth and build rapport. There are three key ways that brands can activate their communities. First, engage advocates to **amplify** their stories and ideas, to grow your community of support. By utilizing a spectrum of engagement, you can expand how you promote your ideology to advance your mission. Filling the content pipeline with stories invites communities to share those big ideas, both with one another and the wider world. Second, invite advocates to **volunteer**. Giving people the chance to get involved directly builds commitment and encourages community "practice," allowing members of the community to feel good about giving of themselves. And, finally, call on your community to **vote** for what they believe, whether via a survey or a national election. Once your audience is engaged, there are three primary ways to raise money:

offer goods or services for purchase, solicit direct donations, and empower your advocates to raise money
themselves. Together these six actions can increase engagement and impact for mission-driven brands.

## Action #1: Amplify Your Brand Idea

In 2011, a group of researchers at Rensselaer Polytechnic Institute showed that only 10 percent of a population
need be convinced of an idea for it to become the majority view.[74] A so-called "committed minorities" of more
than ten percent actively engaged in promoting an idea
can create a critical mass of support that leads an idea to
spread quickly. For this reason, ideology, message, and
story are vitally important. As we have explored, clearly
defining what you want people to understand and believe about your brand is the first step to empowering
others to amplify your mission. While a tendency towards "clicktivism" has led to accusations of laziness on
the part of younger generations, it is helpful to see idea
amplification not as an end of itself but as a positive gateway to more committed action.[75] While insufficient to
generate the commitment and resources needed to enact
change, encouraging new fans to amplify your stories
and ideas can generate positive visibility and grow your
community of committed brand advocates.

In 2016, some help from Russia and a strong values-based
narrative ensured that idea amplification and penetra-
tion weighed heavily in Donald Trump's favor. While
the Clinton campaign's policy-focused message was

overpowered by the paranoid, nonsensical narrative of "her emails," Trump's simple (if improbable) campaign promises created narratives that were easy to share and understand. Whereas working for the Clinton campaign, I was forced to resort to my personal story to motivate advocates and volunteers; Trump supporters were empowered with three-word stories disguised as chants: Drain the Swamp! Lock Her Up! Build the Wall!

If you have successfully followed the first four steps in the method—Ideology, Identity, Message, and Story—you are already set up to empower advocates to amplify your brand. The stories you have developed to amplify certain values to specific segments of your audience are just waiting to be shared. It is up to you to make sure those stories are well-told through the appropriate medium and easily discoverable via your social media channels, your email marketing, and your events. Content amplification is an effective way to test someone's support for your cause and to cultivate their increased engagement.

## Action #2: Volunteer for a Cause

Another way you can call your community to action is by inviting your advocates to give of their time. Volunteering for a cause you care about has two distinct benefits. First, it provides the human-power to advance the organization's mission. While deploying volunteers requires internal systems of selection and management, an investment in those systems typically pays off many times over in the free labor those volunteers provide. Second, volunteering initiates a positive reinforcement cycle for volunteers, themselves. Showing up in person (or online) to provide support makes the impact of the mission that person supports both real and tangible. Getting their hands dirty also effectively exposes the volunteer to the challenges and opportunities an organization faces, which can motivate your advocates to increase their financial generosity as well.

Research has also shown that volunteering has positive psychological benefits. Adam Grant's research on giving shows that volunteering is a meaningful way of contributing to society that can make you more successful, energized, and engaged in your life and work. [76] When it comes to fundraising, those who regularly show up to volunteer are also more likely to donate. Volunteering provides a twofold benefit: the time spent benefits the organization, and the exposure to the organization's mission helps justify their increased support. By participating directly in advancing your mission, your volunteers gain motivation to use all of the resources available to them to make your work possible.

During my time as a field organizer, I witnessed firsthand the clear commitment of so many people who volunteered to help elect Hillary Clinton. From seventeen-year-old high-school girls to seventy-year-old retirees, dozens of people regularly showed up to register voters, knock on doors, and make phone calls to recruit still more volunteers. In some ways, the staunch commitment of our volunteers to show up again and again, day after day, to do the grueling work demanded by twenty-first-century campaigns, made our defeat that much harder to stomach. However, for every volunteer who came back repeatedly, there were five who showed once and were never seen again. Our high "flake rate" provided evidence that while volunteering can be a motivating form of brand engagement, it has its limits. Successful volunteer efforts rely heavily on the structure of community—people, purpose, place, practice, and progress—to ensure volunteers maintain their commitment. Without a strong feeling of common connection and shared purpose, volunteer commitment can flag, undermining your ability to achieve your goals.

## Action #3: Vote for What You Believe In

Some might argue that voting is lower on the spectrum of engagement. How, you might ask, can checking a box on a piece of paper be more significant than writing a check for thousands of dollars? First, perhaps it helps to define what voting actually entails. Most notably, people vote in political elections to determine the people who will represent our interests in government. But voting happens in less important ways, too. You might ask your constituents to choose one of a number of products as their favorite or to identify one of a few graphics they like best. Even completing a survey is voting in a more open-ended way.

Casting a vote rides on the question "Why should I care?" Your advocates must believe that by the simple act of checking the box on the online form—or their ballot—they are initiating real and tangible change. This belief demands that you take steps to consult constituents before asking them to vote, not in ways that assume the answer, but in ways that are open-ended and advisory. It can be tempting to assume you know what your constituents want, in which case you say what you *think* your advocates want to hear.

A timeless adage of fundraising holds true:

*If you want advice, ask for money. If you want money, ask for advice.*

If you want to motivate people to contribute financially to your cause, it can be helpful to ask their opinion on your mission and its impact. With elections, the threshold for consultation is even higher. Your advocates must feel assured that their leaders clearly understand their priorities and beliefs so that when they cast their vote, they can trust their chosen representative to steward the change they wish to see.

In 2016, the Clinton campaign neglected to create buy-in among its diverse constituents. The strategy assumed "true-blue voters"—those who had voted for Obama in the past two elections—could be trusted to turn out and vote for Hillary Clinton in sufficient numbers for her to win where it mattered. Campaign rallies were focused on motivating the most avid supporters, often trying (and mostly failing) to get attendees to volunteer. The campaign overlooked the need to build deep ties of connection and trust, assuming that voters would feel their obligation to vote the same side of the ticket they had for the past decade or more. In the four weeks before the election, our efforts shifted from registering new voters to turning people out to vote. Florida's two-week early voting period meant that people began voting in late October. Our efforts to help people make a plan to vote—deciding where and when they would do so—assumed people wanted to do so. In the end, our failure to understand people's need to see the impact of their vote was the Clinton campaign's undoing.

## Action #4: Buy and Sell for Good

Buying and selling have driven the currency exchange of the world for millennia. I give you money and you give me value in return. For decades, nonprofits insisted that charitable giving was a necessary foundation of their *raison d'etre*, but in recent years, many mission-driven organizations have extended their impact through cause marketing schemes and fee-for-service business models. PYXERA Global is a prime example of a 501(c)3 nonprofit organization that operates primarily as a fee-for-service consultancy in its collaboration with Fortune 500 corporations.

The give-one get-one model, like that offered by TOMS Shoes and Warby Parker, the online glasses retailer, offers the buyer the chance to buy one product for themselves while simultaneously—and invisibly— purchasing a product for a faraway person in need. For the right customer, this might seem like a good way to recruit a would-be brand advocate. Evidence has shown, however, that at least for shoes, pushing free products into developing countries creates distortion effects that ultimately do more harm than good.[77]

Increasingly, however, organizations have begun to leverage traditional business models directly for social good. Philanthropic support might subsidize social enterprises that employ low-income or otherwise disadvantaged individuals, but the organization is designed to produce goods for purchase. Al Kawtar, a nonprofit handcraft collective in Marrakesh, Morocco, employs disabled women who would not otherwise be able to find employment. Lonely Planet and others promote their wares both for their quality and for the buyer's experience of supporting a good cause.[78] PazPeru is a nonprofit organization in Arequipa, Peru, which provides housing and support for women and children who are victims of domestic violence.[79] Women who stay at the facility also have the chance to work in the clothing factory, which manufactures branded fleeces and outerwear for companies in the region. Companies who buy from PazPeru can purchase high-quality garments knowing that their products offer vital support for women in need. More familiar to most, Girl Scout cookies are another popular product many people buy for a cause.

While "products for good" have become increasingly popular, using a fee-based model to reach revenue targets can be challenging work. It demands a clear business model and robust marketing infrastructure that is often dramatically different from the communications mechanisms required for more traditional fundraising. Transactional engagement, however, can be a comfortable way to get people to open their wallets, which can pave the way for future charitable giving. What's more, branded products can help further amplify your brand.

In 2016, red MAGA hats became the quintessential commodity of Trump's America, while T-shirts inscribed with I'M WITH HER and DEAL ME IN became the battle cry of Hillary's coalition. Often the Clinton campaign would send fundraising emails that led with a campaign product promotion. While completing a product purchase—with a credit card already in hand—the form invited the purchaser to add a donation to the order, turning a product purchase into a giving opportunity.

## Action #5: Endurance for Dollars

While many people struggle with asking others for money without due justification, physical feats have in recent years become an effective way to encourage advocates to raise money from their immediate community of friends and family. According to Classy, a fundraising platform, the 1969 Church World Service Hunger Walk in Bismarck, North Dakota, was among the first walks for charity in the United States.[80] Since that time, the ways that people use physical endurance to demonstrate their belief in a cause have multiplied. The Race for a Cure has helped the Susan G. Komen Foundation raise $2 billion, which it has invested in breast cancer research and prevention.[81] Cycle for Survival is a stationary bike race that funds the Memorial Sloan Kettering Cancer Center's work to treat rare cancers. Many different types of organizations host dance-a-thons—twenty-four-hour dance parties—to raise support. In the summer of 2014, the ALS ice-bucket challenge captured the imagination of Americans. For weeks, videos of people dumping buckets of ice water on their heads, and, of course, the hilarious antics that followed, overwhelmed Facebook and Twitter. The challenge helped the ALS Association raise $115 million *in one summer*, which subsequently enabled them to invest $96 million in new research to address that devastating disease.[82]

Organizations whose work addresses physical ailments are perhaps best positioned to take advantage of physical-endurance fundraisers, but other brands can learn from this model of engagement. Fundraising leading up to an anticipated event is helpful because it builds urgency. Creating an endurance component—even if it is only three hours on a stationary bike—helps people feel as if they are part of the collective efforts of a larger whole. While people may only give $25 or $50 to a friend's fundraiser in advance of an event, this contribution is a gateway to future support. By investing in the cause—even if only because a good friend has asked—that organization has now grown its community of support, adding to its rolls a new donor who can be cultivated and solicited in the future.

In a perverse way, political-campaign management in America has become its own kind of endurance sport. Our campaign team worked seven days a week, fourteen hours a day, with a late start at noon on Sundays. Supporters from both sides were willing to wait in line for hours for the chance to attend a candidate's rally, live, while the candidates themselves hurried from plane to motorcade, hopping from rally to fundraiser. While neither campaign capitalized on the traditional endurance-for-dollars construct, the demands on our field organizers and volunteers alone demonstrated the fortitude required to run a campaign. Rather than downplaying the physical feats required to advance your mission, celebrate them. Create opportunities for advocates to pledge financial support for efforts that coincide with structured endurance efforts on the part of you, your team, and your volunteers.

## Action #6: Philanthropic Support

Charitable giving is a crucial driver of mission-driven work, but an astounding number of organizations fail to make the case before asking for support. So many leaders set out to vaguely "fundraise" without stating definitively how much money they are seeking to raise or a clear statement of why. While each prospective donor segment warrants a different strategic approach, a few universal best practices are worth mentioning. First, you must define how much money you are seeking to raise, the timeframe in which you seek to raise it, and the benefit those funds will provide, once secured. This logic informs every successful capital campaign ever undertaken. Smaller nonprofits may not have the same need to raise hundreds of millions of dollars to erect buildings, but they can learn from the success of many large fundraising departments. A five-year campaign to raise $10 million will almost certainly work better than ad hoc efforts to raise an undefined sum.

In addition to creating a clear structure as to why and how fundraising targets will advance an organization's mission, you must also cultivate that support by educating prospective backers about your track record of success and your vision for future impact. Rarely does a perfect stranger to a cause immediately, upon first contact, say, "Why yes, let me write you a check for $10,000 right now!" Many donors will start with small gifts that serve as unconscious tests of both mission achievement and operational sufficiency. If I give an organization $100, what happens? How do they respond? If I give them $250, what then? Each of us has a different threshold for what a "small" or "large" gift is—many wealthy Americans write several $1,000 checks a year without expecting much cultivation in return. A surprising number of leaders fail to think of fundraising as a multiyear spectrum of engagement. In the campaign to raise $10 million in five years, a new donor may give a gift of $250 in year one, but with regular stewardship and engagement, you could cultivate them toward a donation of $10,000 or more in year five.

In 2012, I wrote an article for the *Chronicle of Philanthropy*, "Five Things Charities Do That Turn Off Young Donors Like Me." Many nonprofits typically commit five errors when engaging Millennial donors: i) talk at me instead of with me; ii) send me junk mail; iii) stay silent about your business model; iv) undervalue my capacity to give, and; v) fail to ask for my advice.[83] The prevailing point is that young donors will not be young for long. Instead of categorically limiting how we see people and their potential generosity, it is best to invite them into the highest levels of engagement. By treating every person as a potential six-figure donor, fundraisers may increase their workload. However, they also dramatically increase the potential generosity advocates can express to advance the mission.

Most importantly, perhaps, you must make the case for how a donor's support will advance your cause. In the case of the Hillary Clinton campaign, the campaign inundated supporters with daily emails prognosticating doom, demanding that you "chip in $25 right now" to stop whatever stupid initiative Donald Trump had proposed. Even as a field organizer on the campaign's payroll, I received solicitation calls from the finance team in New York. These appeals were divorced from both ideological vision and campaign strategy. Sadly, to this day the Democratic Party maintains the same feckless approach.

Live events, such as conferences and elections, create time-bound urgency that can help brands achieve their fundraising goals. Overuse of the state of emergency created by an impending deadline can, however, come at a cost. When urgency appeals promise doom that never arrives, it is natural for advocates to become skeptical. Instead of asking someone to "pitch in $5 right now" every single day, you might consider asking someone to contribute $600 this year with a credit-card payment of $50 a month. By engaging a donor to make a more strategic gift, the brand also has permission to offer that donor a higher level of stewardship and engagement. The donor who gives $50 a month this year might increase her support to $75 a month the next year and perhaps to $100 a month the year after that. Suddenly, the would-be $5 donor is now contributing $1,200 a year to your organization, and asking for a two-part gift of $5,000 does not seem so out of reach. In this way, you can build a virtuous cycle of increased engagement based on a clear strategic aspiration, rather than trying to keep the wolves at bay with incremental "emergency" actions.

Often our diagnosis of the failure to take action responds to the symptoms of circumstance rather than the underlying cause:

"We've seen a real decline in engagement from young people."

"Moms are consistently choosing our competitor's product."

"Other organizations are outraising us in their annual campaign, two-to-one."

In my experience, the questions that typically follow these types of diagnostic proclamations are almost always the wrong ones, laying blame on the constituent rather than rigorously evaluating the brand's role in failing to inspire engagement. Inevitably, the failure to spark action traces back to an apparent gap in the Heptagon Method.

In the days that followed the election, my mind reeled with theories and ideas of what, if done differently, might have changed the outcome. The media and Democrats alike were in search of the one thing they could blame. Russia, James Comey, and pervasive misogyny quickly emerged as the front-runners, along with the accusation that the campaign had been "badly run." This last shortcoming rankled me, as I had watched so many people almost kill themselves to achieve their assigned metrics and objectives. In my view, the *execution* of the campaign strategy was practically flawless. The assumptions underlying that strategy, however, were arrogant, short-sighted, and ultimately wrong.

I reflected on my experience communicating on behalf of mission-driven organizations. What actions, taken in sequence, lead to a desired outcome? I had witnessed many rush to the end result—*action*—without first laying the groundwork for motivation, and call it failure. But with deeper cultivation, I realized that organizations can more successfully inspire supportive communities prepared to take action. When I thought about my grandmother Marjorie's admonition to "pull up your socks and get on with it," I realized that when organizations clearly prescribe exactly what they want you to do, people are a lot more likely to do something.

## Three Bonus "Spark" Factors

In his book *The Tipping Point*, Malcolm Gladwell describes the three key factors needed to spark a trend that takes hold.[84] You may also want to consider these in addition to the foundational elements described above.

First, Gladwell articulates the Law of the Few, which explains that not all people are created equal. Some brand advocates are Connectors, whom Gladwell describes as those with "a special gift for bringing the world together."

These are the people who know *everyone*, regardless of community or interest area, and who can ensure an idea disseminates quickly to reach the right people. Others are Mavens, "information brokers, sharing and trading what they know," who provide the validation that an idea is a good one. Finally, Salesmen are persuasive individuals who have the indescribable ability to make people want to agree with them. In the making of a movement, they are critical in turning skeptics into believers. Gladwell's Law of the Few insists that all three types of people must be involved in advancing an idea for it to take root and spread.

Second, Gladwell's Stickiness Factor alludes to the qualities of an idea that make it memorable. Similar to the advice in Chapter 6 about using stories to make your brand pop, if an idea is overly complex or terribly boring, people are unlikely to take up the cause, despite your best efforts. Humor, rhyming, and radical simplicity are three ways brands can make their ideas more memorable. If your brand is not achieving its goals, consider ways to increase stickiness to increase engagement.

Lastly, the Power of Context plays an important role in action as well. There is such a thing as right-time-right-place magic, which influences how resonant an idea is for your target audience. Would the #MeToo movement have cascaded so boldly without the revelations of Harvey Weinstein's misdeeds? Without the *Access Hollywood* tape? Or the Women's March? Who can say?

With no prior exposure to what they do or why, brands with a mission face the challenging task of convincing people to believe that progress is possible. Unavoidably, cultivating advocates to believe in a cause takes time. Motivating your potential allies to see their responsibility to contribute to the change takes more time still. To encourage your followers, shine a light that they can flock to, to fuel and sustain the passion of your would-be advocates. Whether you are trying to make an idea spread, working on raising millions of dollars, or motivating citizens to vote, keep them coming back to the light for solidarity and inspiration.

## CHAPTER 10

# The Heptagon Method at Work

*"The squaw on the hippopotamus is equal to the sum of the squaws on the other two hides."*
–Dad Joke

When I was in the sixth grade, beginning to learn geometry, my father told me a joke. "Once, there was an Indian chief," he said. "And one day, as he was walking a visitor through camp, the chief pointed out a squaw sitting on a hippopotamus hide. He said she weighed 300 pounds. He showed the visitor two more squaws, each sitting on deer hides, and each weighing 150 pounds. Do you know the moral of the story?" he asked. I listened, not sure what deer hides and Native Americans had to do with geometry. "The squaw on the hippopotamus," he said, beaming, "is equal to the sum of the squaws on the other two hides." The punchline was accompanied by fatherly jazz hands. "Come on! It's the Pythagorean theorem," he prodded. "The square of the hypotenuse is equal to the sum of the squares of the other two sides?" I groaned, rolling my eyes.

The Heptagon Method is not a mathematically proven formula like the Pythagorean theorem, but it is a systematic strategy for brand development that can help many types of organizations, but especially mission-driven organizations, expand their brand's reach and influence. Having moved through the method in depth in each of the past seven chapters, it becomes clear how the steps sync together to create a coherent pathway for brand development:

1. Ideology
2. Identity
3. Message
4. Story
5. Experience
6. Community
7. Action

Brands that will benefit most from this method fall into one of three categories: new, underperforming, or broken. Each presents challenges and opportunities to leverage the Heptagon Method for greater clarity and impact. Whereas the previous chapters in this book HAVE examined each of the seven steps individually, this chapter explores how each step relates to the others to create a comprehensive transformation in how an organization communicates. For more established brands, dysfunction or confusion in the early steps of the method can have trickle-down effects elsewhere.

## Accelerating Impact: Using the Method to Power New Brands

New brands belong to organizations or initiatives that are just getting started. As founders find their point of impact, they realize that building an identity to support their efforts will be key to their product or service's market impact and success. In this case, the Heptagon Method serves as a generic roadmap, instructing the sequence of actions you should take to develop and amplify an idea, initiative, organization, or brand.

## Brand Foundations: Ideology, Identity, and Message

Many founders are not marketing experts themselves, so the number of unknown factors to address outnumber those for which they have a ready approach. In this sense, the method seeks to make the process of brand evolution transparent, to empower founders with the capacity to DIY, to do so efficiently and effectively, or to know when to hire help. Many founders may find it necessary and impactful to define their own impact. Hiring a graphic designer to help develop a strong visual identity is typically a worthwhile investment.

## 1. Ideology

At this phase, there is sometimes confusion as to what a brand *is*, what "brand" actually *means*. Recently, I spoke with a new founder who responded to this very question. While some organizations treat brand at the surface level, caring only about its visual appeal, the best brands are those with a deeper identity and personality. For this reason, the archetypal branding method helps organizations go further than "what looks good?" or "what sounds good?"—where it is easy to end up by default. "Who do we want to *be*?" and "Who do we want to *become*?" are the most important questions to ask when choosing the archetypes and defining the mission, vision, values, and personality for a brand.

## 2. Identity

When developing the brand identity, naming is often the biggest challenge faced by new brands. An explicit name that states exactly what your organization does may be appealing, but more evocative brands offer greater flexibility and typically endure better over time. One choice is to find a name that is suggestive, like Some Spiders Studios, a brand inspired by *Charlotte's Web*, which points to the importance of childhood stories and the interconnectedness of all things. These days, many brands favor a portmanteau approach, blending two words into one to combine their meaning. Pinterest (Pin + Interest), Netflix (Internet + Flicks), Intel (Integrated + Electronics),

Verizon (Veritas + Horizon), and Acroyoga (Acrobatics + Yoga) are all examples of portmanteau brands.

While some founders intuitively know what they want to call their brand, others struggle with finding the "right name." Some start out with a misnomer and recognize the need to make a switch before they get too public. And that's okay! Many brands go to great lengths to ensure their brand is "likable," sending surveys to listservs to ask people to vote, or eliminating options that people who are distant from the brand dismiss. Many founders want that perfect identity that elicits a "Wow! Cool!" response. The truth of a name, however, is far more important than its wow factor. Does the name convey the core elements of the identity? Overthinking how to name your brand can sometimes get in the way of actually putting the brand to work.

### 3. Message

Message compels you to define whom you are trying to reach and what you need to convey to inspire that audience segment. Many new brands try to be universally relevant. The more clearly defined the target customer, however, the more effective an organization will be in meeting that customer's needs. While the ideology stage defines what the brand stands for, and why it exists, the message phase offers the chance to adjust the brand's voice for each audience. For a new brand, being diligent about completing the brand foundations is a critical step in setting up the organization for future success. By establishing your ideology and identity and understanding its relevance to your audience, you create the groundwork for effective future amplification and engagement.

### 4. Story

Story strategy is an important next step in brand evolution. While slated as the fourth step, story is an ongoing effort that sustains the brand's voice and visibility. Prioritizing story strategy is an important step in amplifying a brand's impact and vision. Your message will not amplify itself. You must determine the best medium by which to reach your audience and the storytellers who are most likely to inspire them.

---

## Brand Activation: Experience, Community, and Action

Once the first four elements are in place, it is time to turn to the challenge of brand activation. How can you leverage experience to foster community that will motivate your brand advocates to take action? Ideally, you will begin with the end in mind. What are the actions that will deliver the most value to your brand? What are the strategic capabilities you need to develop to empower your brand advocates to advance your impact? Then design an experience that your target audience will enjoy and which will foster their buy-in and engagement. It is important to create the community structures into which you will invite your advocates before the event takes place.

### 5. Experience

Hosting experiences is an expensive undertaking, but it almost always yields positive results. While the inter-connectedness of today's world often leads us to believe we can accomplish as much by way of the Internet as we can in person, there is special magic that emerges when people come together in one place for a shared moment in time. Use the time with your advocates to help them develop a connection to one another and to your cause.

### 6. Community

Building communities at this stage can be challenging. Sustained engagement requires a clear container that people can be a part of, one that also allows people to play an active role in evolving the community's core purpose. Your brand advocates must gain some value from show-ing up and at the same time feel empowered to deliver value back to other members of the community.

### 7. Action

And, lastly, your call to action must be clear and per-suasive. What, exactly, are you asking people to do? For early stage initiatives, this is often as simple as, "Buy our service or product!" but leverage the ideology to make this action more meaningful. Why should I care about buying this product or service? What is the value I'm delivering to the world by doing so? Having ready

answers to these questions will help convince your advocates to act.

---

## From Good to Great: Reinventing Underperforming Brands

Underperforming brands face a different challenge. In
this case, a brand has likely existed for some time, but
audience engagement has diminished or brand confusion has increased. Sometimes this is simply a matter
of a shift in context. For example, organizations that
were relevant before the dawn of the Internet may face
challenges in adapting themselves to a smartphone-
dominated world. Those working on issues of race
and gender empowerment now face a new paradigm
of "wokeness" with #MeToo and #blacklivesmatter
that demands new positioning. For underperforming
brands, the Heptagon Method serves as an evaluation
rubric by which brand leaders can identify points of
weakness in the brand's communications infrastructure and take action to reinforce them. Adjusting one
element of a brand can recalibrate the other parts of a
brand's marketing strategy.

Ask your constituents what they think your mission and
vision are—if you receive vastly varied responses, that
is a good indication your ideology lacks clarity. When
senior leaders get stuck asking, "What's our 'why'? Our

purpose?" it is time to re-evaluate the brand's vision and values.

A name that is too generic or inaccurately explicit (think "CDC Development Solutions" back in Chapter 4) can lead to identity confusion. Do you have an extraordinarily high bounce rate on your website? This metric is a good indicator people land on your homepage because they are looking for something else, like people searching for "CDC" and abandoning Citizen Development Corps' website because they were actually looking for the Centers for Disease Control. Many brands struggling with a confused brand identity struggle to summon the courage to change their name. Naming is difficult, and competition abounds. A bad name will rarely completely hinder an organization's ability to achieve its mission, but a sharp new identity can be like fertilizer on underperforming roots.

Once you reinforce your ideology and identity, you must re-evaluate your message. While the general demographics of your audiences may be well known, "audience personas" help brands clarify the fears and desires of each audience segment. Understanding what inspires and provokes your audiences provides an important foundation for the tailored communication of new ideology. Often this means emphasizing key values or themes to audience segments that have specific interests or concerns.

Some brands may have a well-established ideology but fail to amplify their core beliefs to the world. Without a story strategy to reach the right audience segment, it can be challenging to mobilize your brand advocates. Once you have clarified and validated your ideology, identity, and message, it is time to develop the storytelling channels that build connection with your brand advocates. Curating experiences to inspire your community to take action flows naturally at this stage.

Before the launch of its new brand, PYXERA Global struggled to communicate effectively about its mission and work. As the organization pivoted away from USAID contracts toward private-sector engagement, the "Development Solutions" part of its name quickly became more of a liability than an asset. The organization made a few anemic attempts at fundraising, with little return. Client cultivation took an inordinate amount of time and investment in personal relationships. Barriers to effective communication limited the organization's reach and impact. While core programs were still aligned to its mission, the actual words used to express any aspect of the brand were opaque and confusing.

From 2012 to 2015, the brand's position improved dramatically. The development of the new brand took the better part of a year. While it took time to build consensus among both internal and external stakeholders—clients, staff, and senior leaders—doing so ensured that the ideology represented the organization's diverse experiences and history. Defining the mission, vision, and values before developing a new logo ensured that the new brand identity conveyed the right qualities. Choosing a new name and developing a new logo was an involved process; defining brands that endure means taking the time required to get it right.

The launch of *The New Global Citizen* magazine was the first exercise in effective storytelling focused on important themes for PYXERA Global's key constituencies. Focusing the publication on strategic themes—Global Pro Bono, Enterprise Development, Impact & Innovation, Citizen Diplomacy, and Leadership—amplified clear messages that targeted specific segments of the brand's audience. Creating a storytelling platform to which members of the broader community were invited to contribute further increased PYXERA Global's brand visibility and the role it played in creating a culture of sustained collaboration on the new frontier of purposeful global engagement. Over the course of three years, our team published hundreds of stories, dozens of which appeared in the quarterly print compilation, ensuring that these narratives were both broadly shareable online and catalogued in a lasting analog format.

Because the organization had already begun to use events to convene its key constituents, it was easy to use one of these experiences to launch the new PYXERA Global brand.[85] The success of that conference made way for the first Global Engagement Forum the following year, which shifted the conversation from its previous focus on global pro bono and corporate volunteering to a broader mandate, focused on how corporations can advance the Sustainable Development Goals. By 2016, the PYXERA Global brand was so strong that the independence of *The New Global Citizen* (which we had launched before the new brand existed) no longer made sense. In 2016, *The New Global Citizen* became the Global Engagement Forum: Online, building from the annual event to create the foundation for PYXERA Global's online brand community. The live event takes place every eighteen months, while conversations continue online in webinars, Twitter chats, and online articles between gatherings.

Transforming PYXERA Global's brand helped solidify its action focus. The Global Engagement Forum now focuses on solvable problems within the context of the Sustainable Development Goals (SDGs), shifting the attention and resources of corporations toward issues where their sustained commitment can yield guaranteed results.[86]

In many ways, the most challenging step in the process took place before the rebranding ever began: organizational consensus about the problem. Many times, organizations with years of experience and name recognition among their core constituents shy away from the opportunity to undertake a comprehensive rebranding, fearful of the ramifications of choosing a new name.

The devil you know is less scary than the devil you don't. CDC Development Solutions was an ineffective brand that constrained the organization's ability to advance its mission. Deirdre White realized that the confusion created by the name and the absence of a well-amplified ideology was holding the organization back. She took the time needed to align both staff and board leadership to the transformation. When the naming process began, everyone agreed that a more elusive, evocative name would better serve the organization's future growth and adaptation over time. By strategically strengthening the brand's foundations and investing in sustained strategies for storytelling and brand experience, PYXERA Global emerged, unlocking new levels of visibility and impact. White's executive leadership was critical to the process and its ultimate success.

Crafting strong brand foundations takes time and care. One story is rarely enough. Ensuring your advocates receive your message demands a sustained commitment to thought leadership and storytelling. Bringing allies together can be done both in person and online, though each progressive experience should demonstrate an innovative step forward. Those convened need encouragement and direction on how to embrace the practice and place in which their community can continue to evolve. People benefit from clear calls to action that will accelerate progress.

At the last Global Engagement Forum Live Event in April 2017, White emphasized the need for diverse partners to work together. "Collaboration takes the head of a sage, the heart of a visionary, and the feet of an explorer," she proclaimed. Finally, the brand archetypes, the very first elements of the brand identified four years prior, had found center stage.

## Facing Full-On Reinvention: Fixing Broken Brands

Broken brands face a unique circumstance. In this case, every aspect of the Heptagon Method is either dysfunctional or underperforming. Does the audience have a neutral or negative impression of the brand's value? Is there a high level of distrust? When a brand is broken, leaders will exert an extraordinarily high level of effort in marketing or fundraising efforts with limited returns.

An emerging cult of personality is a classic characteristic of broken brands. In recent years, nowhere has this been more prevalent than in politics. Throughout this book, I have offered circumstantial comments on my experience as an employee of a Democratic coordinated campaign. Since the campaign's end, my perspective has intensified as I have watched Democratic leaders respond to a devastatingly unexpected (and humiliating) loss. In the current political climate, however, both the Republican and Democratic Parties are confronting a unique brand cataclysm.

In recent years, the Democratic Party has styled itself as the "big tent party of everyone," without actually articulating what that means. Democratic candidates insist on campaigning on policy rather than standing for the values of their constituents. In this environment, repeated losses have become the norm. Whereas the mandate to vote was once guided primarily by partisan affiliation, in recent years parties have come to depend on the personality of the candidate to motivate voters. The charisma of the candidate overwhelms the qualifications of the individual or the importance of party. The Democratic Party's failure to serve the needs of a majority of Americans has undermined its brand standing. Unfortunately, Hillary Clinton had her own brand liabilities that ultimately undermined her broader appeal.

By the fall of 2016, evidence that Russia was attempting to influence the outcome of the US election had begun to emerge. But as Clinton's campaign manager Robby Mook admits, his efforts to sound the alarm were met with skepticism and dismissed as conspiracy theories.[87] Both the campaign's minimalist approach to external communication and the success of the disinformation campaign conspired to effectively frame Hillary Clinton for her "lies" and "deceit." In this environment, members of the media interpreted Mook's attempts to spread the truth about Russia's interference as the proliferation of falsehoods.

Perhaps the "Hillary Clinton" brand broke under the weight of reputational sabotage. Some percentage of the voting public believed in Hillary Clinton as an individual. Many, however, grudgingly voted for her, not because they believed she represented their values and aspirations, but because they saw her as the "lesser of two evils." While the Clinton campaign succeeded operationally in many ways, neither "Democrats" nor "Hillary Clinton supporters" were a strong enough coalitions of brand advocates to carry the election in the places where it counted most.

While Democrats had claimed to be the big-tent party of the everyman for decades, their actions spoke louder. Bernie Sanders, for all his flaws, had found the Democrats' Achilles' heel, and capitalized on it to great effect, emphasizing the party's hypocrisy. As a candidate, Hillary Clinton spoke ad nauseum about the detailed policy proposals she hoped to enact once elected, attempting to dumb them down for the public, and, in the process, making herself even less relatable. The campaign's communication relied on the false assumption that the American electorate cares most about policy as the grounds on which it elects its representatives.

Most voters, however, are not motivated to show up at the polls based on their understanding of a candidate's proposed jobs plan and foreign-policy resolutions. They vote based on how the candidate makes them *feel*. Can they trust this person to represent their best interests? Does the candidate share their values? Donald Trump had more ably activated an aggressive and vocal segment of the voting public, making them feel validated and heard, affirming their hate for immigrants and promising to assuage their fears with the prospect of a Muslim ban and a border wall. Any policy wonk could see these promises were not intended to be practical; they were meant to inflame the passion of their intended audience.

Meanwhile, the Democratic Party had been breaking its promises—losing elections it should surely have won, increasingly dependent on money from corporate interests. The party, having forsaken the needs of everyday people for those of Washington lobbyists, had compromised its morals, and as a result, broken its brand.[88] The opposite of hate is not love but apathy, a malady rampant in American politics, made worse by consistent failures and inconsistent values.

The Democratic Party had lost sight of what it stands for, and, in the process, allowed manipulation and subterfuge to undermine its standing. How does a brand come back from such devastation? In the days after the election, I thought a great deal about this question. What would it take to reimagine what the Democratic Party stands for?

In my view, redefining what the Democratic Party stands for did not mean a trite new tagline, like the one rolled out by the party in the summer of 2017—what Jamil Smith fittingly called "a whitewashed retread of DNC talking points."[89] The implication was third-order rebranding, not just changing the logo or slogan, but redefining *why* the party exists and the goals it seeks to address (besides "the working class," "jobs," and winning).

While many Democratic politicians continue to pay lip service to "Democratic values," it is not clear that Americans have a shared notion of what that phrase means. Somewhere between the Civil War and the battle for African American civil rights, the neoconservatism of Bill Clinton's presidency, and the war between "Progressives" and "Liberals" (not to mention the undermining propaganda of such conservative rabble-rousers as Rush Limbaugh and Alex Jones), we all lost track of what it means to be a Democrat. The ideology of the Democratic Party: gone.

If you are (or were once) a self-proclaimed Democrat who has grown disillusioned with the party's defiance of any definable moral compass, then you may be satisfied with this diagnosis. If you are one of the few Americans who remains staunchly committed to the party, in spite of its missteps, perhaps this discussion has left you disgruntled. If you consider yourself more of a disillusioned Republican feeling your party shift startlingly to the right, perhaps you are simply fed up with all this talk of the Democrats whom you have considered to be foolish nincompoops since time before memory. (It is perhaps a measure of the era that being Catholic, Jewish, or Protestant once held the same tribal fealty as political-party membership seems to hold today.)

My analysis in these pages has focused on the Democratic Party because it is the institution I know best, both as a lifelong member and a former employee. Based on this exposure, I have done my best to offer a thoughtful analysis of the brand. Simply because of its broad national visibility, it is an accessible reference point for those seeking to understand broken brands to avoid breaking them in the first place.

When a brand loses touch with its purpose, the trust of its stakeholders begins to flag. In 2017, United Airlines suffered two highly visible incidents of employee misconduct that brought the brand's values into question. The public responded with general distrust—assuming the worst rather than extending the brand and its ambassadors the benefit of the doubt. A loss of trust and credibility between a brand and its audience is the best evidence a brand is truly broken. "United should change their name before it's too late," someone quipped on Twitter. Changing a name, however, will not address the absence of clear conviction and purpose.

When ideology is unclear, it can be most helpful to begin by asking prospective or current constituents to offer their insight and personal experience as a guide. The best forms of inquiry assume that you do not know the answer to the question you are asking, leaving the door open to diverse responses. If the Democratic Party truly wants to reclaim its national standing, its leaders will need to listen to both liberals and independents from across the nation, to understand how they are and are not serving the values and priorities of their constituents. Before her 2000 bid for the US Senate, Hillary Clinton undertook a listening tour across the state of New York to understand the needs and concerns of New Yorkers. A similar approach across the country could yield significant benefits. By first understanding the human experience of everyday Americans and their shared beliefs, the party could remake itself in that image, a beacon of servant leadership.

Fixing both underperforming and broken brands is difficult, tedious work. Leaders must possess a clear conviction that something is wrong and resolve to allocate the resources to address the problem. Often, organizations with a tight budget will choose to work with what they have rather than invest in efforts to fix the underlying issue. Only addressing the symptoms of a problem without confronting its root cause, however, typically yields diminishing returns. The corollary of "If it ain't broke, don't fix it" is, "If it's broken, for the love of God, fix it!" Brands that choose to suffer under the yoke of dysfunction and confusion do so at their peril.

I recognize, however, that summoning this conviction is a difficult first step. Fear—of failure to achieve anything, or, worse, of committing an egregious error—can be a stranglehold on progress. It can be tempting to maintain the status quo rather than take action. The Heptagon Method provides a clear path out of the paralyzing fear of being stuck in the status quo, toward a determined future state. Do this first, then that, *then* the other thing. Do not start with fundraising or product positioning. Instead, begin with values, mission, and vision. Why are you here? What is the impact you seek to have? Define a North Star and then proceed toward it by all means available. Inherent in this process is a strong degree of trust in the face of fear. Trust that if it is not yet good, it is not the end, and that we all deserve better than the grueling reality of wading through the swamp of a damaged existence. Follow the steps in sequence. It gets better. I promise.

## CHAPTER 11

.

# Conclusion

*"We are the ones we have been waiting for."*
—June Jordan

On the morning of November 9, 2016, I was overwhelmed with emotions, encumbered by recent events, and unsure of what to do next. In the days afterward, my grandmother Marjorie's ghost always seemed near at hand, asking, "When are you going to pull up your socks and do something?" I thought back on the campaign and reflected on where we had gone wrong.

I saw clearly all of the places where confirmation bias had guided beliefs, from headquarters all the way down to our field office in Pompano Beach. I wondered how any of us had arrived at the arrogant conviction that the strategy used to elect a young, charismatic, and popular black man running on a vision for change could also elect an older and in many circles wildly unpopular white woman on an incumbent's coattails.

How foolish we had been to believe that organizing strategies that had worked in 2012 would yield the same success four years later.

I thought regretfully of how hard we had worked, only to lose, and realized that a system predicated on people working eighty hours a week for less than minimum wage is already broken. Working for months with no days off leaves no time to consider an alternative approach. The false urgency of the "house on fire" prevented us from asking questions and shielded our superiors from having to respond to concerns. We brought a clipboard to a street fight. Our opponents showed up with proverbial machine guns.

Perhaps most importantly, in the face of an arrogant conviction that exhausting ourselves in service to an outdated campaign plan was an infallible strategy, we failed to ask and answer the most important question: *Why are we here?* At no point did we have the opportunity to clarify our ideological conviction and validate our shared purpose.

These challenges, accounts of which have been threaded throughout this book, are not impenetrable. Nor are they specific to the 2016 Hillary Clinton campaign. Over my career, four key tenets have guided my approach to brand strategy and communication: i) question everything; ii) stay human-centered; iii) champion purpose, and; iv) reimagine possible.

## Step 1: IDEOLOGY

Ideology is the bedrock of any mission-driven organization's brand. If you want to engage for change, it starts here. Whether you are seeking to develop a new brand, rebrand an organization with a long history, or fix a broken brand, it makes sense to clarify and (re)commit to the ideology that motivates your work. Ideology depends on three core components, each of which is underscored by a question:

- **Vision:** What is the outcome you seek to achieve, and what will be accomplished once you do so?
- **Mission:** What actions and activities will you undertake to arrive at that desired outcome?
- **Values:** What guiding principles will you honor in pursuit of your goal?

Every person who contributes to advancing your mission should clearly understand the answers to these questions, which together articulate your **Brand Promise**, the core commitment you offer your brand advocates. Such clarity of purpose helps to define the **Personality** you want to radiate outward, defining how your community of brand advocates will perceive you in the process. To better understand how ideology advances progress and impact, and how it governs the formation of brand identity, check out Chapters 3 and 4.

## Step 2: IDENTITY

The moment an ideology becomes a brand is critical to converting a big idea into a banner for action. For legacy brands like PYXERA Global, an antiquated identity can hinder potential impact. Defining your brand name and visual identity—the logo, colors, and fonts that represent your ideology—can be resource-intensive. While it often takes more time than you expect, the investment in a new brand identity almost always pays dividends.

Three factors drive the successful creation of a new identity:

- **Talent:** Having the right mix of people in place is critical to an identity transformation. You need a creative agency that understands you, an internal champion to manage the process, high-level approval from your board of directors, and active engagement from both clients and staff. Scrimping on any of these things is unlikely to improve the ultimate outcome.
- **Time:** Identity projects are complicated. Developing a well-crafted name and logo means allowing your team to take the time they need to get it right. While time pressure will ensure the project does not become the enemy of the good and that the project gets done, having the flexibility to push deadlines when warranted and extend the schedule for completion can open up necessary space for productive creativity.

- **Transformation:** Most important of all is to welcome the opportunity for fundamental change. Too often, rebranding can devolve into incremental changes from an existing identity because long-time stakeholders are fearful of the repercussions of losing hard-earned brand equity. Compassionately silence those critical skeptics and embrace the chance to go boldly in a new direction under a new banner for meaningfully impact.

For an example of radical identity transformation, re-visit Chapter 4.

## Step 3: MESSAGE

To successfully spark a movement for change, you need to understand both what you stand for and how your core beliefs resonate with your audience. Without a messaging strategy, your outreach can become unspecific and ineffective, failing to inspire your audience. What is more, certain aspects of your ideology may inspire different segments of your audience. Just as you may not wear the same set of clothes on a date as you would to Sunday lunch with your grandmother, it is natural to emphasize different elements of your brand to inspire your advocates effectively. Grounding targeted messaging in empathy can help ensure that the rest of your engagement strategy will resonate, and ultimately motivate action.

Three steps form the basis of effective messaging: empathize, strategize, amplify:

- **Empathize:** "Get out of the building" and test your ideology with actual stakeholders. By investigating what resonates, you can develop a detailed empathy map.
- **Strategize:** Craft values-based messages that activate your advocates based on the issues and ideas about which they feel most passionate.
- **Amplify:** Use your message as a framework from which to identify and tell stories that will catalyze action.

To read more about how to "get out of the building," develop stakeholder empathy, and craft an effective message, return to Chapter 5. Together, steps 1–3, which include Ideology, Identity, and Message, form the foundation of a strong brand, the bedrock from which to activate your audience to engage for change.[90]

## Step 4: STORY

Humans are naturally motivated and informed by narrative. Stories are the most powerful and effective way we convert information into understanding. When it comes to engaging for change, stories are both an efficient way to help your advocates internalize key information about your ideology and an important foundation from which to foster support for your work. In Chapter 5, you can read more about how a message forms the basis of story strategy.

Three core stories form the foundation of public narrative, which, according to Marshall Ganz, are necessary to motivate communities to act: the Story of Self, the Story of Us, and the Story of Now:

- **The Story of Self:** This story examines the choice moments you have faced that have led you to this work. It combines the challenges you have faced with the hard-fought victories you have won to define how and why you have arrived at your ideology.
- **The Story of Us:** This story defines the parameters of your community. It explains what makes your advocates distinct from others, and what defines the basis of your in-group. It builds on the characteristics of community explained in Chapter 8.
- **The Story of Now:** This story explains why action in this particular moment is fundamental to progress and your theory of change. It emphasizes the need to act and the payoff for doing so.

In Chapter 6, you can read more about the stories of Self, Us, and Now, and find the seven-step framework designed to help less-experienced storytellers communicate their experiences with less effort and more impact.

## Step 5: EXPERIENCE

Shared moments have powerful potential to catalyze collective identity. *E Pluribus Unum*: out of many, one. Whether attending a live theatre production, a rally, a conference, or a town hall meeting, I enter a space as me, alone, and together we leave as us, transformed by the inspiring moments we have shared. Capturing this magic requires simultaneously managing nuanced details and big-picture strategy. As the examples in this book have shown, drawing on the power of convenings to advance your cause demands placing human engagement at the center of your strategy and building out from there.

To plan an effective convening, focus on three core components: programming, production, and participation:

- **Preparation:** Dynamic events require a clear-cut goal supported by a three-pronged strategy: to entertain, to educate, and to motivate. Once the key themes are defined, they must be messaged effectively and reiterated throughout the program. Incite your constituents to show for you. Ensure that the substance of your agenda is rich and provocative. The core elements of your ideology should be on display and the pillars of your community should be evident. Where possible, provide tailored experiences for each segment of your audience.

- **Production:** Do not let a faulty projector or a low-battery microphone detract from your audience's experience. Ensure that lights, sound, set design, and timing support your overall goals and attendee experience. Prepare your speakers for what they will encounter on stage. Make sure they are prepared to amplify the message you seek to convey and the experience you wish to curate.

- **Participation:** Tim Brown said it first: "All of us are smarter than any of us." Using event formats that empower participants to crowdsource session topics and facilitators maximizes buy-in among attendees. Taking advantage of the people who show up by engaging their talents increases their motivation to remain engaged well after the event. Provide the structure and support to help people connect with like-minded collaborators, learn from one another, and plan for action. By empowering your audience, you can enhance the enjoyment and inspiration of everyone present and spark future action.

To understand how events foster collective cohesion and how to curate an event that can spark change, revisit Chapter 7.

## Step 6: COMMUNITY

Belonging is one of the most powerful motivators of human engagement. When people share a common identity, they will more easily collaborate toward shared action.

While communities often seem to emerge organically, they typically arise out of sociological behaviors that motivate cohesion and engagement. Community often results from the energy of a shared moment in time, the natural in-group that forms from colocation and common experience.

Beyond the people who must participate and the purpose they serve, three core pillars nurture sustained engagement within a group: practice, place, and progress:

- **Practice:** Seth Godin's maxim, "People like us do things like this," guides how people engage. It is up to you to define the rituals that bind your community together, to help people understand what they must do to participate, and the value they will gain by doing so.
- **Place:** The world is a big, confusing place. People need a clear understanding of where and when they will find others with whom to engage in your community's practice. Acroyogis find each other in parks during warm weather; StartingBloc Fellows find each other on Facebook. Define where your community will congregate, whether in physical or virtual space.
- **Progress:** Apathy is to passion what futility is to progress. To motivate your community to sustain their engagement, you have to demonstrate how their commitment connects to your ideology, how their actions advance your vision. By linking your

vision with their practice, you encourage your community to build momentum for your cause.

You can read more about the sociological underpinnings of community and belonging in Chapter 8. To understand how to call your community to take action, you can revisit Chapter 9.

## Step 7: ACTION

Many leaders set out to call people to act without first paving the pathway for them to do so, so I recommend that you address the first six steps before proceeding to this point. Once your supporters are ready to take action, there are three key ways you can engage them to help advance your cause: broadcast, bankroll, and ballot:

- **Broadcast:** Empower advocates with stories they can amplify to their friends and families. Encourage them to express their personal experience of your brand, its mission, and their participation in the community. Engage them in a two-way conversation that expands your visibility and invites engagement from those who are not yet involved.
- **Bankroll:** Call on your allies to underwrite your work. Explain in specific terms how their financial support will make your future vision possible. Empower them to buy and promote your products, to use endurance for dollars, fundraise on your behalf, and to give directly to advance your cause.

- **Ballot:** Give your supporters a stake in determining your brand's future. Ask their advice through polls and surveys. Engage them in decisions that merit democratic processes. In the case of political campaigns, empower them to vote for leaders who will advocate for your shared ideology.

To explore different forms of action and their benefits in more detail, check out Chapter 9. To understand how the sequence of the steps in the method leads to greater empowerment and activation among advocates, read Chapter 10.

---

## The Road Ahead

Sometimes November 9, 2016 feels a million years away in my memory, as if it happened in an otherworldly space-time continuum that I can no longer fully remember. Other days, it feels viscerally proximate, as though the actions of America's forty-fifth president are my fault, a direct result of my failure to knock on enough doors, recruit enough volunteers, or turn out enough voters.

On some level, my rational mind knows the failure of 2016 is not individual but collective. I know that many people above my paygrade made far more dire mistakes—failures of arrogance rather than effort. I understand that there are foreign powers hellbent on disrupting the stability of modern democracy in order to increase their own power. I also appreciate how a culture of digital distraction and siloed information consumption permeates the American psyche, undermining our best efforts to create a concerned and engaged electorate. All of this offers little more than cold comfort. To list the factors of influence outside my control is to acknowledge my powerlessness.

Recently, a community organizer I know posted a quotation on Facebook:

*I always wondered why somebody didn't do something about that. Then I realized, I am somebody.*

Hope for our future depends on the conviction of everyday Americans to see our collective power for what it is. Each of us is somebody.

One week after November 8, 2016, I wrote the following note to the volunteers who had worked alongside me in the lead-up to the election:

*We confront moments in life that look like the end. Sometimes they are mountain peaks, other times cliff edges, often the beach. In these places, life comes to a standstill. You look down at your feet, up at the sky, and appreciate the world around you. As we approached the end of this harrowing presidential campaign, many of us were physically and mentally prepared for such a moment. The race was hard-fought, and we were all ready for it to be hard-won. Mother Nature, God, or the universe—whoever or whatever you believe in—often has a way of playing tricks on us when we take too much for granted.*

*As I sit and marvel at the end result and the aftermath of this campaign, it is hard to imagine how so much generous hard work could lead to a loss. This campaign beat records—we deployed more volunteers than ever in the history of American politics. On November 7, across the nation, this campaign knocked on 11 million doors and spoke with 20 million voters over the phone. Though the result is not what we hoped, I will be forever grateful and honored that I was on the front lines fighting this fight and that I got to do so by your side. Some of you came from far and wide, and others came from across town, but universally, the diversity and commitment of this incredible group of volunteers, who came back again and again, always looking for how to do more, inspired me to get up, to fight through exhaustion, to do my job better than I did it yesterday, every single day. Thank you, from the bottom of my heart, for everything you gave to this campaign.*

*Today, America finds itself at a crossroads. Nate Silver, the infamous founder of FiveThirtyEight, pointed out what a difference two percentage points would have made, how the outcome would have been different if one in every 100 voters had chosen differently. Today,*

*America is truly a divided nation, split among those who feel disenfranchised by "politics as usual," who are inspired by Donald Trump's call to upend the status quo, and those who believed in Barack Obama's vision for a better future back in 2008, who only wanted the progress of the last eight years to continue marching forward.*

*We thought we had reached an end, but in fact, we confront a new beginning, a moment in which we cannot take for granted all that Barack Obama has accomplished. Instead, we must stand by and defend it, and closely examine the failings of the institution that was unable to gain the political support to continue his legacy. This fight will be long, and likely frustrating. It will depend on the willingness of good people like you to continue to dedicate yourselves to its pursuit. As we now know all too well, victory is never guaranteed. But fighting for progress, for a better future—the blood, sweat, and tears—are always worth it.*

It is remarkable to reflect on the clarity I had just six days after Hillary Clinton's historic defeat, much of which remains the anchor of my vision for the future and the beliefs that underlie my conviction to do this work. I am grateful for the chance to have served on the front lines of American democracy, in arguably the purplest state in America (one we would later learn was on the forefront of Russia's attempts to undermine American democracy). I remain awed and inspired by the committed volunteers to whom this book is dedicated, who showed up when the going got tough, again and again. Having summoned the strength to run the last mile I wrote about in those final days, I have realized that was simply the first marathon of many.

Other things have shifted. I see now that fighting for anything depends on a shared understanding that someone will win, and someone will lose. By being inside of the machine advancing Hillary Clinton's candidacy, I gained a better and deeper understanding of the "losers" who the past two decades of political leadership—including that of Bill Clinton and Barack Obama—have left out in the cold. Fed up with being overlooked and underserved, many Americans have reliably seized every opportunity to vote for change. By getting outside of the elite echo chamber of Washington, DC and New York, I had the chance to engage firsthand with those Americans who are hungry for a new kind of politics.

It is not just electoral politics that are broken by a winner-take-all paradigm, but the core guarantee of dignity at the heart of the American dream. Changing America's future from one of despair to one of hope will require more than incremental changes in strategy or investment. To make tomorrow look different from today, we must stop doing what we have always done to stop getting what we have always gotten. We must embrace the chance to fundamentally change how our systems of governance, economics, and justice work together to promote dignity for every American. We cannot count on government, business, or nonprofits to solve this problem alone. We are going to need to design and execute the systemic changes required to achieve these outcomes together.

Where to start? How does one begin to reimagine the world in which we live?

First, you must realize that within you lies the seed of hope. There is no one coming to save us from ourselves. There is no one with the answer to our prayers waiting to rescue us from the rising tide, both literal and proverbial, of impending doom. You are the one we have been waiting for. This prospect may seem daunting and impossible. Reading this sentence may cause you to put down this book, roll your eyes, and shake your head. If *that's the case,* you think, *then we are all totally screwed.*

However, there is some good news. You are not alone. All of us are a collection of somebodies with the power to do something. When we join together in our conviction to do so, the world suddenly looks different. We are no longer David against Goliath. You are Voltron, the Power Rangers, and the Transformers rolled into one. Our powers combine to make the impossible both imaginable and achievable. Progress may be slow. There will be many disappointments on the road ahead. But when we work together, all manner of things become possible.

Perhaps you are already well on your way to creating the change you wish to see in the world, in which case, congratulations are in order! You have searched through the treasure trove of life's mysteries and found the one priority that has earned your commitment and dedication. You may already be surrounded by the allies who share your conviction and who will journey with you as you advance your cause. For you, I hope this book provides a useful framework from which to increase your impact and accelerate your progress.

For those of you who have not yet found your cause or your squad, fear not. Your allies are out there, waiting for you. How will you find your fellow travelers on this journey? Hold up the light of your conviction. The path to shared ideological clarity begins with inquiry. Talk (and not just on social media) to those with different experiences and perspectives, and search for the common threads of understanding that connect you. Call on your friends, your neighbors, the person standing next to you in line at the grocery store, your FedEx delivery person, your corner-store clerk. Invite them to join you in dialogue. Ask: "What are the values we share?" and "What is the future we want to work together to create?" The answers to these questions form the basis of your ideology, the starting point in the framework from which you can invite others to engage for change.

This work is challenging. Sparking and sustaining movements with the potential for impact demands acknowledging our confirmation bias and making a committed effort to look beyond what we already know (and believe) to be true. We must slow down long enough to ask pointed questions and listen—*really* listen—to the answers. This means putting the question of conviction—*Why are we here?*—at the heart of our work. Doing so may feel uncomfortable at first. Human minds are not naturally inclined to embrace uncertainty. But sit with it. Get comfortable being uncomfortable. Embrace the chance to listen to others, to hear how they have felt overlooked and marginalized by the systems that have failed to serve us. Use curiosity and questions as your guide. Hear them not with judgment, but with compassion, and ask, "What would it take for you to thrive?" This question is where a human-centered approach begins. By making the lived experience of our fellow humans the primary source material for progress, we can imagine new solutions to the challenges we face. By shifting our approach from what it has traditionally been, we unlock the possibility of creating something fundamentally different and new. We begin to pave a path toward transformation.

Rome was not built in a day. Progress takes imagination, dedication, and, most of all, time. Believing in the possibility of something better is often the hardest part. When we show up for one another and elevate our shared conviction, we begin to actualize the power of collective action, which can provide the momentum needed to break through the status quo and shape a radically different future.

I look forward to our continued collaboration on the future still waiting to be created. Together, we can ignite the flame of common promise that burns within each of us.

Are you ready? Go ahead. Make history.

# ACKNOWLEDGEMENTS

So many people have made *Purpose Power* possible, and I am grateful to all of them. I would like to sincerely thank:

Jailan Adly, Deirdre White, Melissa Mattoon, and Laura Asiala, whose vision, commitment, and encouragement made possible so many opportunities for learning and impact.

Hila Mehr, for her curious and impressive ability to spark connections that have shaped my life, and, as a result, this book.

Alice Chin, Steve Darr, Drew Cogbill, Kimberly Kagan, Marisa Sullivan, Kate McClellan, and Kristine Sloan, who believed in my ability to engage for change, and in so doing shaped the arc of my career.

Esme Hoffman and Andrew Chapman, who believed in this idea from its inception; Emily Crookston, whose dedication and insight shaped the narrative into its present arc of inspiration; and JuLee Brand, who made it a reality.

Ellen Erway, for her extraordinary command of the English language and her willingness to use it in service to this book.

My husband, Andrew, for the constant love and support that made this book possible.

Genevieve Switz, who bred into me the conviction to question convention and defy expectations.

Most especially I am grateful to Fred Bonner, who witnessed and encouraged each stage of narrative evolution with patience, care, and enthusiasm. Thank you for teaching me to look toward the light, even in moments of darkness. Only by standing on your shoulders can I help others see more clearly what is possible.

# ABOUT THE AUTHOR

**ALICIA BONNER NESS** inspires mission-driven leaders and organizations to engage for change. She is a community organizer, brand strategist, and event producer passionate about helping people find common cause. After more than a decade working in the social sector, she founded Heptagon Productions, a brand-activation agency through which she serves mission-driven organizations in civic engagement, democracy reform, and social justice. A LUMA Institute–certified human-centered design facilitator, Alicia uses a unique blend of open ideation and design activation to help individuals and organizations uncover their shared conviction to pursue their higher purpose. Educated at Johns Hopkins University, Barnard College, and Miss Hall's School, Alicia learned her most important life lessons before the age of ten. She lives in Brooklyn, NY, with her husband.

---

## Chapter 2

1    Graff, Garrett/ Wired Magazine, February 2018 https://www.wired.com/story/mueller-indictment-russia-attack-us-democracy/

2    Kony 2012: https://goo.gl/gJyMT4

3    The Arab Spring: https://goo.gl/bmcpeB

4    Freedom Riders: https://goo.gl/Td0u85 and Civil Rights Act: https://goo.gl/D5MmYm

5    Salt March: https://goo.gl/jNgKp

6    Everytown for Gun Safety: https://goo.gl/BpmKOM

7    Ness, Alicia. Firebrand: https://goo.gl/KusMHa

8    Ideology definition. Merriam-Webster Dictionary: https://goo.gl/zyr81I

9    Sinek, Simon: How Great Leaders Inspire Action TEDx: https://goo.gl/dQ6pr6 and Start with Why: https://startwithwhy.com

10    Mirror Neurons and Empathy: https://en.wikipedia.org/wiki/Mirror_neuron#Empathy

11    Marsh, Jason. Greater Good, March 26, 2012: https://goo.gl/kHPtsJ

12    Lamm, Claus and  Jasminka Majdandžić. *Elsevier*: The role of shared neural activations, mirror neurons, and morality in empathy – A critical comment p. 19 https://goo.gl/m22xbJ

13    Ganz, Marshall. 2011. "Public Narrative, Collective Action, and Power." In *Accountability Through Public Opinion: From Inertia to Public Action*, eds. Sina Odugbemi and Taeku Lee: 273-289 Washington D.C: The World Bank. https://goo.gl/CBXJav

14    Double Dutch Insider, December 14, 2016. http://doubledutch.me/blog/psychology-behind-successful-hands-event/

15    Gino, Francesca and Michael I. Norton, May 14, 2013 *Scientific American* https://www.scientificamerican.com/article/why-rituals-work/

16    Meet Up: https://en.wikipedia.org/wiki/Meetup_(website)

17    Philips, Matthew, Minority Rules: Why 10 Percent is All You Need July 28, 2011, Freakonomics https://goo.gl/s2y1qB

## Chapter 3

18    Human Rights Campaign Background http://www.hrc.org/hrc-story/mission-statement; http://www.hrc.org/hrc-story/our-victories; http://lawecommons.luc.edu/cgi/viewcontent.cgi?article=1355&context=pilr

19    Drutman, Lee. *Politico*: November 15, 2016. https://www.politico.com/magazine/story/2016/11/mobilization-only-politics-2016-214456

20    Broockman, David and Joshua Kalla. *Science*: Durably reducing transphobia: A field experiment on door-to-door canvassing  08 Apr 2016: Vol. 352, Issue 6282, pp. 220-224. DOI: 10.1126/science.aad9713 https://goo.gl/f36wyx

21    Denizet-Lewis, Benoit. *The New York Times*: April 7, 2016. https://goo.gl/ge1eNw

22    Rozin, Randall. *Journal of Brand Strategy.* Autumn 2012: Brand promises and a practitioner's unified theory of brand management https://goo.gl/e4o8Bf

23    Heptagon Brand Quiz: https://goo.gl/vDAXxY

## Chapter 4

24    Hurst, Aaron. *The Purpose Economy:*  How Your Desire for Impact, Personal Growth and Community Is Changing the World. 2014. p. 64

25    B Corporations Background https://www.bcorporation.net/

26    Jungian Archetypes https://en.wikipedia.org/wiki/Jungian_archetypes

27    PYXERA Global Background: https://sage.pyxeraglobal.org/pyxera-global/who-we-are/vision-goals-and-attributes/

28    PYXERA Global Background: https://www.pyxeraglobal.org/who-we-are

## Chapter 5

29    Lean Startup: https://www.leanstartupmachine.com/about

30    Human-Centered Design: https://en.wikipedia.org/wiki/Human-centered_design

31    Business Model Canvass: https://en.wikipedia.org/wiki/
Business_Model_Canvas

32    Empathy Map: https://www.solutionsiq.com/resource/
blog-post/what-is-an-empathy-map/

33    Clinton, Hillary, Methodist parable:  Do all the good you
can, for all the people you can, in all the ways you can, for as long
as you can. https://twitter.com/hillaryclinton/status/77402426235
2941057?lang=en

34    Desilver, Drew. Fact Tank. August 7, 2018:
http://www.pewresearch.org/fact-tank/2018/08/07/
for-most-us-workers-real-wages-have-barely-budged-for-decades/

35    Ries, Eric. The Lean Startup: How Today's
Entrepreneurs Use Continuous Innovation to Create Radically
Successful Businesses. 2011. https://www.amazon.com/
Lean-Startup-Entrepreneurs-Continuous-Innovation/
dp/0307887898

36    Ries, Eric. How Modern Companies Use Entrepreneurial
Management to Transform Culture and Drive Long-Term Growth.
October, 2017. http://www.thestartupway.com/

37    Patagonia CSR: http://www.patagonia.com/corporate-
responsibility.html

38    Patagonia CSR: https://www.patagonia.com/save-our-
public-lands.html

39    Patagonia Mission Statement: http://www.patagonia.com/
company-info.html

**Chapter 6**

40    National Democratic Institute. #NotTheCost Stopping
Violence Against Women in Politics Guide https://www.ndi.org/
sites/default/files/Public%20Narrative%20Participant%20Guide.pdf

41    Cooke, Ed. The Guardian. January 14, 2012. https://www.
theguardian.com/lifeandstyle/2012/jan/15/story-lines-facts

42    Ganz, Marshall. 2011 p. 283 "Public Narrative, Collective
Action, and Power." In Accountability Through Public Opinion: From
Inertia to Public Action, eds. Sina Odugbemi and Taeku Lee: 273-289
Washington D.C: The World Bank. https://goo.gl/CBXJav

43    Ganz, Marshall. 2011 sic Tailor 1989 p. 91

44    Ganz, Marshall. 2011, p. 282

45   Naidu, Laveen. Global Engagement Forum. https://www.pyxeraglobal.org/dance-diplomacy-connecting-the-global-human-experience-through-dance/

46   Ganz, Marshall. 2011. "Public Narrative, Collective Action, and Power." In Accountability Through Public Opinion: From Inertia to Public Action, eds. Sina Odugbemi and Taeku Lee: 273-289. Washington D.C: The World Bank. http://nrs.harvard.edu/urn-3:HUL.InstRepos:29314925

47   Grant, Adam M., Elizabeth M. Campbell, Grace Chen, Keenan Cottone, David Lapedis, Karen Lee: Impact and the art of motivation maintenance: The effects of contact with beneficiaries on persistence behavior. Elsevier https://goo.gl/2bUayi

48   Knowledge@Wharton https://goo.gl/fsM7iE "Impact and the Art of Motivation Maintenance: The Effects of Contact with Beneficiaries on Persistence Behavior," published in the Elsevier journal of Organizational Behavior and Human Decision Processes

49   http://nrs.harvard.edu/urn-3:HUL.InstRepos:29314925 p. 285

50   Ganz, Marshall. 2011. Ibid. http://nrs.harvard.edu/urn-3:HUL.InstRepos:29314925 p 286

51   White, Deirdre; Global Engagement Forum: https://www.pyxeraglobal.org/danger-victory-laps/

52   White, Deirdre; Global Engagement Forum: https://www.pyxeraglobal.org/development-sector-needs-new-words-better-ideas-dramatic-innovation-build-better-world/; https://www.pyxeraglobal.org/2015-un-must-balance-effort-aspiration-ratify-sustainable-development-goals/

53   White, Deirdre; Global Engagement Forum: https://www.pyxeraglobal.org/can-shared-value-surpass-the-promise-of-csr/

54   http://nrs.harvard.edu/urn-3:HUL.InstRepos:29314925

55   Ganz, Marshall. 2011 p. 288

56   Ganz, Marshall and Hahrie Han. The Nation, June 22, 2016: https://www.thenation.com/article/what-hillary-clinton-can-learn-from-bernie-sanders-and-donald-trump/

57   Ganz, Marshall. 2011 p. 289

## Chapter 7

58    Gino, Francesca and Michael I. Norton. *Scientific American*, May 14, 2013 https://www.scientificamerican.com/article/why-rituals-work/

59    Norton, Michael I. and Francesca Gino. "Rituals Alleviate Grieving for Loved Ones, Lovers, and Lotteries." Online First Publication, February 11, 2013. doi: 10.1037/a0031772 http://www.people.hbs.edu/mnorton/norton%20gino.pdf

60    Barber, Nigel. Is Joy Communal? https://www.psychologytoday.com/blog/the-human-beast/201605/is-joy-communal

61    Bandura, Albert: Modeling and Observational Learning. http://professoralbertbandura.com/albert-bandura-modeling-and-observational-learning.html

62    Experience Design: https://en.wikipedia.org/wiki/Experience_design

63    Public-Private Partnership Forum: https://goo.gl/sQxskg

64    PYXERA Global SDG Venn Diagram https://goo.gl/fS6v6E

65    Bains GS, Berk LS, Daher N, Lohman E, Schwab E, Petrofsky J, Deshpande P. "The effect of humor on short-term memory in older adults: a new component for whole-person wellness." https://www.ncbi.nlm.nih.gov/pubmed/24682001

66    Brown, Tim. *Change by Design: How Design Thinking Transforms Organizations and Inspires Innovation.* 2009. https://www.amazon.com/dp/B002PEP4EG/ref=dp-kindle-redirect?_encoding=UTF8&btkr=1

## Chapter 8

67    Acroyoga: https://en.wikipedia.org/wiki/Acroyoga

68    AcroCity Jammers: https://www.facebook.com/groups/286455668168891/

69    Katherine Wertheim, Werth-It Consulting http://www.werth-it.com/

70    McMillan, David W. and David M. Chavis Journal of Community Psychology Volume 14, January 1986 Sense of Community: A Definition and Theory; George Peabody College of Vanderbilt University p. 11 https://goo.gl/qMdiyC

71    Sprinks, David. The Community Manager: November 19, 2013 http://thecommunitymanager.com/2013/11/19/the-psychology-of-communities-4-factors-that-create-a-sense-of-community/

72    McMillan, David W. and David M. Chavis. Ibid. p. 11 https://goo.gl/qMdiyC

73    McMillan, David W. and David M. Chavis. Ibid p. 19

**Chapter 9**

74    Rensselaer Polytechnic Institute. July 25, 2011: Minority rules: Scientists discover tipping point for the spread of ideas. https://phys.org/news/2011-07-minority-scientists-ideas.html

75    Clicktivism Definition: https://www.techopedia.com/definition/28184/clicktivism

76    Adams, Susan. Forbes. April 1, 2013: https://www.forbes.com/sites/susanadams/2013/04/01/7-ways-that-generosity-can-lead-to-success/#1dfa3cb510c5

77    Tom's Shoes: https://www.economist.com/blogs/freeexchange/2014/10/economics-toms-shoes

78    Al Kawtar: https://www.lonelyplanet.com/morocco/marrakesh/shopping/al-kawtar/a/poi-sho/1509176/1316370

79    Paz Peru: http://www.pazperuong.org/

80    Harel, Terri. Classy. https://www.classy.org/blog/the-evolution-of-the-charity-runwalk-and-the-road-ahead-2/

81    Race for the Cure: https://ww5.komen.org/RaceForTheCure/

82    Ice Bucket Challenge: http://www.alsa.org/fight-als/ice-bucket-challenge.html

83    Ness, Alicia. *Chronicle of Philanthropy*. November 11, 2012. https://www.philanthropy.com/article/5-Things-Charities-Do-That/155841

84    Gladwell, Malcolm, *The Tipping Point: How Little Things Can Make a Big Difference.* https://goo.gl/RvqRBZ

**Chapter 10**

85    PYXERA Global Public-Private Partnerships Forum: https://www.pyxeraglobal.org/pyxera-globals-icv-conference-public-private-partnership-forum/

86    PYXERA Global Solvable Problem Challenge: https://www.pyxeraglobal.org/solvable-problem-challenge/

87    Mook, Robby, Washington Post, December 2018 https://goo.gl/Vqdkvp

88    Newton-Small, Jay. *Time Magazine*, July 27, 2016. http://time.com/4425343/dnc-hillary-clinton-lobbyists-donations/

89    Smith, Jamil. Vanity Fair, Hive. August 11, 2017: https://www.vanityfair.com/news/2017/08/why-the-democrats-better-deal-is-political-suicide

**Chapter 11**

90    If you are unsure about your organization's ideology, identity, and message, you can take the Heptagon brand quiz to learn more about where to begin: https://goo.gl/vDAXxY

CPSIA information can be obtained
at www.ICGtesting.com
Printed in the USA
BVHW081409250319
543610BV00030B/2053/P